PENGUIN BOOKS

OURS

F. E. Peters, who continues "to view life through Jesuit eyes and greet it with Jesuit laughter," is now Professor of Islamic Studies at New York University.

OURS

The Making and Unmaking of a Jesuit

F. E. Peters

PENGUIN BOOKS

Penguin Books Ltd., Harmondsworth,
Middlesex, England
Penguin Books, 625 Madison Avenue,
New York, New York 10022, U.S.A.
Penguin Books Australia Ltd, Ringwood,
Victoria, Australia
Penguin Books Canada Limited, 2801 John Street,
Markham, Ontario, Canada L3R 1B4
Penguin Books (N.Z.) Ltd, 182–190 Wairau Road,
Auckland 10, New Zealand

First published in the United States of America by
Richard Marek Publishers, Inc., 1981
Published in Penguin Books 1982

LIBRARY OF CONGRESS CATALOGING IN PUBLICATION DATA
Peters, F. E. (Francis E.)
Ours, the making and unmaking of a Jesuit.
Reprint. Originally published: New York: R. Marek,
c1981.
1. Jesuits. 2. Peters, F. E. (Francis E.).
3. Jesuits—New York (State)—Biography. 4. New York
(State)—Biography. I. Title.
[BX3706.2.P47 1982] 271'.53'024 [B] 82-9864
ISBN 0 14 00.6317 X AACR2

Printed in the United States of America by
R. R. Donnelley & Sons, Inc., Harrisonburg, Virginia

Nostris

Contents

I	VOCATION	15
II	REGULAR ORDER	38
III	THE RELIGIOUS LIFE	59
IV	OBSERVANCE	76
V	MEDITATION AND OTHER TRIALS	92
VI	SPIRITUAL THEATER	112
	1. BROTHER GELLER IN CHAINS	112
	2. HOLIDAYS ABROAD	115
	3. LUDI VEL LABORANDUM	121
	4. FIRST-CLASS RELIC	130
VII	DELIVERANCE	139
VIII	THE PERENNIAL PHILOSOPHER	163
IX	THE DEVIL'S PARADISE	193

OURS

It pleases the Jesuits to call themselves "Ours." Ours were not to own property, were to regard the Superior as the instrument of the will of God and were to have as little as possible to do with Externs, all those who were not One of Ours. I am an Extern of long standing now, but for nine years I was One of Ours and dwelled in that remote country where Jesuits trained and planned for their assault on the World.

I presently live in the World, a forbidding and yet enormously attractive place from which there is no return. There are still some of Ours about, not as many as there used to be, and presumably the assault goes on as planned, though with what success I do not know. We chat about other things, I and Ours, when we chance to meet, without acrimony and often in that winning worldly style that Jesuits cultivate to charm the hell out of Externs and win their Immortal Souls. They are ambivalent but satisfying conversations, those random moments here and there, because I was schooled in the same discourse, and the rich ambiguity of encounter between the Worldly Jesuit and the Jesuit Worldling gives pleasure to both.

I can only speak of the past. Ours loved to be Ours. Their rules refer to the Jesuits as "this least Society," an expression almost paralyzed with irony. If there is a "least Society" in the bosom of Mother Church, it was assuredly not, on the Jesuits' own reckoning, the Society of Jesus. It must be some other confraternity pursuing its own imperfect vision of the religious life. Some were fitfully admired by Ours in the manner of a connoisseur smiling upon a picturesque ruin, once glorious things like the Benedictines or Dominicans that had fallen into decay. The more remote the ruin, the greater the pretended respect: Carthusians, whom no one had ever seen, were thought to be obscurely worthwhile, but the Franciscans, whatever their imagined service to the Church in the past, were by now unspeakable. Others were mere cartoons: the dimly single-minded like the Passionists; shamelessly self-promoting entrepreneurs like the Maryknollers; the unnumbered hordes of helot brutes posing as Brothers, Christian, Irish Christian, Marist or whatever; and your parish priest who at least owned up to his inferior status and so won from Ours the same grudging respect that the physician grants to the dentist but withholds from the insolent chiropractor.

Whoever they were, they were not to be compared to Ours. We were the Major Leagues, and the unanimously shared opinion was that everyone recognized it, even the Pope and, more importantly, even the World. Years later, long after turning in my pinstriped uniform with "Ours" emblazoned across the chest, the most modest and casual allusion to a Jesuit past still brings the shamelessly satisfying acknowledgment that this guy had once carried a bat to the plate in the Bigs.

It is a world long gone. St. Andrew on Hudson is now the Culinary Institute of America, and for all I know Loyola Villa may be a Club Med. Nor am I entirely sure what Ours are doing these days by way of keeping themselves up to the mark, but it likely has little to do with what I experienced or thought about during those nine years among Ours. A contemporary Jesuit would doubtless find much of it quaint or perhaps even barbarous or scarifying. No matter. It was there long enough for me to enjoy it and even to feast upon it. I too loved being One of Ours, and in the only way that was then possible. I am not certain I would still love it. Too worldly. Them, not me.

I

Vocation

It seemed like a good idea at the time, and so on July 30, at
an age before I discovered anxiety, I coolly sat down in
the New York Central coach that would carry me to
Poughkeepsie, New York, and to a place I had never seen,
the Jesuit Novitiate of St. Andrew on Hudson. I am not
very sure where ideas, good or bad, come from—my old
Jesuit skill at the discernment of spirits has long departed—but I have thought a good deal about the genesis
of this particular idea, with its nine years of consequence.
I was a good Catholic: I believed it all and I tried to avoid
sin. I was neither a particularly devout nor virtuous
young man. I was not making any particular progress in
the spiritual life, but I was picking up some speed in the
low sexual minors in which an eighteen-year-old Irish
Catholic boy played at that time.

If this doesn't sound like Jesuit material, it was. I was
also a bright and articulate adolescent who got good

grades without raising a perceptible sweat, who could write English prose, parse Latin, read French, make movies, edit a newspaper, play football, easily charm elders and convince peers. It was this happy combination of aptitudes and inclination that had originally plucked me out of a Bronx parish and set me down, via a competitive exam, at Regis High School, the premier Jesuit prep school in the United States.

It was a quite perfect moral universe, that Irish Catholic corner of the Bronx which even today rests serene in the twilight of its severe orthodoxy. God, Church and parents shared each other's authority in defining, explicating and policing a univocal value system to which we, its childish subjects, were firmly bound. It was a consort of ventriloquists, with all mouths moving in such precise harmony of movement and matter that no one of us could tell who was actually speaking. The priests and nuns of Our Lady of the Assumption parish handled the Keys of the Kingdom with as much right as Saint Peter, and my parents pronounced on behalf of God as unabashedly and assuredly as the Pope himself.

What they were preaching, God and His two sets of infallible and interchangeable vicars, was a simple creed; Obey and Know Thy Place. The objects of obedience were those selfsame preachers of the Word, and in that trinitarian moral theology, disobedience to one was disobedience to all. The exact location of my eventual "place" was still obscure, but it was presently that of a subject, haloed round by the cardinal middle-class virtues of respect, submission and responsibility and gaudily festooned with guilt. A certain Hell awaited the recusant, and so from the age of six to sixteen I weekly confessed disobedience with all the fervor of a recidivist alcoholic.

Eight miles to the south and a world away from this Jansenist cloister in whose dark interior I groped toward adolescence was Regis High School, where for four years I was taught by Jesuit priests and young men undergoing their training for the priesthood in the Society of Jesus. It was Regis and its Jesuits who reordered my Catholic universe. God still rested remote in His Heaven, but the Universal Church was now enlarged by the presence of a blinding Jesuit sun, which cast those lesser Bronx asteroids into a pitiful penumbra. More, they delicately but effectively separated my parents from that harmonious conspiracy of the Word whose protection and asylum they had so long enjoyed. The Reverend Thomas Browne, S.J., smoothly but firmly took the dummy off the ventriloquist's lap.

Tom Browne was not my hero. I may not even have liked him. He was a little too smooth; he tried a little too hard in that way that adolescents are so quick to detect. He was, nonetheless, a revelation. He listened. He sympathized. He encouraged. Here was someone clad in the official clerical black who was willing to concede to my eager spirit that my parents were quite capable of being unreasonable, or silly or mistaken. "Disobedience" passed forever out of my confessional repertoire. And he bestowed upon me something quite new in my still limited experience, self-esteem.

It was only thirty-five minutes by subway from Pelham Bay in the Bronx to Eighty-fourth Street and Park Avenue in Manhattan, but it was an interstellar voyage for all that. Regis, it became immediately apparent, was *my* world and not my parents'; its achievements were now my achievements. And New York was now *my* city. I roamed it day and night with my new friends like the proprietor of a newly inherited estate. It was the purest adolescent bravado perhaps, but it was heady stuff, and it transformed me and many of my contemporaries in a manner they can recall to this day.

The Jesuits took no credit for the World or my debut in it. They approved my harmless flight from the nest, but they were not liming their own nest for me when I alighted. It was I who judged them, closely and carefully, these strange and attractive new creatures. Neither their sanctity nor their piety made the slightest impression on me. Rather, they struck me as the epitome of cosmopolitan sophistication, those men whose vocation it was to renounce the World. Oblivious of the paradox, I admired the Jesuits precisely for their worldliness.

And since I later stood on that other, Jesuit side of the teacher's desk in one of their high schools, I know they must have regarded me in turn and weighed the possibilities of my joining their number. And what they saw in me would be as paradoxical as what I admired in them. At eighteen, a senior in high school, I had neither piety nor devotion to commend me. But I was already what many of the younger Jesuits who taught me were: quick, intelligent, detached and amusing. A winner, and in the unmistakable Jesuit style.

It was a silent courtship; no word of seduction or troth was uttered on either side. But I wanted them. They represented another, new and different life. I didn't particularly want to be a priest or a monk—priests I identified as the men who said Sunday Mass in Our Lady of the Assumption parish and of monks I knew nothing— I wanted simply to be a Jesuit, to be like my wise, intelligent and compassionate mentors in those class- rooms. I said yes, though no question had been asked. Yes, I want to be like you, Mr. Moore, S.J., and Mr. La Bau, S.J., and Mr. Cullen, S.J., and you, Father John O'Brien, S.J.

And they wanted me. They explained to me all that was involved and I listened with all the deaf intensity of a bachelor receiving instruction on the married life. Vows? Why, certainly. Silence? Of course. Long years of study? Easy. A priest forever according to the Order of Melchizedek? Sure. Never mind the terms. I was ready, without condition or reservation, to join their number, to live their life whatever it was.

A vocation is literally a call, a whisper in the case of Socrates, a shout for the early Christians on whom the Holy Spirit descended amidst the clash of cymbals and the roll of supernal drums. That was a simpler and more direct age, perhaps, with better spiritual acoustics. In these latter days the Holy Ghost has become all but inaudible. I heard neither whisper nor trumpet in my ear, no unmistakable summons to leave the World and take up the clerical state. I may indeed have heard a call, a voice not from on high but from deep within myself bidding me exchange my narrow Bronx cloister for the larger, more spacious grounds of the Jesuits. Only by hindsight did I identify it as the working of the Holy Spirit; it was really freedom that was calling.

It sounds curious, or an almost ludicrous miscalculation, the embrace of that regulated, disciplined Jesuit life in the name of freedom. Oddly, it was not. My adolescent perception was correct: my life as a Jesuit was a liberating and enlarging experience from the first day to the last, nine years of it. Its limitations were endurable and its vistas were infinite. Though I would be vowed to obedience, move to a bell and live in the anonymity of a black-robed community, my life at last was in my own hands.

Whatever form it took for the others, I was not the only one in the Jesuit high-school network who had heard the Call. There were nine of us who rendezvoused that late-July afternoon in Grand Central Station: Tom Connolly, Charles Gilligan, Ray Gorman, Tony Houghton, Joe LaBella, Matt Leahy, Bill McGarry, Steve Toland and I, not exactly a catholic representation of the Universal Church, but a pretty fair replica of American Catholicism and its clergy. We were all moderately bright, tolerably virtuous and now visibly nervous, though obviously eager for what then seemed more like an adventure rather than a change of life so absolute as to be unimaginable.

We established ourselves in the club car as if we had never known any other abode and bravely attempted to contrive a debauch out of loud laughter, a few Tom Collinses and a great many Lucky Strike cigarettes. We argued the merits of—what else?—Regis and Fordham Prep and Xavier High School, already our past, and yet we showed only minimal curiosity about each other, oblivious of the strong possibility that we might be spending the next sixty years of our lives in each other's company. And some in their haste to embrace the clerical style already wore black suits and fedoras.

The clothes were not impromptu. Like feckless campers heading into a summer that might last a day or a lifetime, we had been provided with a list of clothes to bring with us, and on it was the black suit and the black hat now being flashed so self-consciously by some. The entire enterprise of my going off from home, family and familiar ways had taken on its first, and perhaps only note of reality a few weeks earlier when my mother and I made our cautious way into Rogers Peet men's store and bought that black suit, black shoes and socks, and a strange token of elegance, a collarless white shirt with French cuffs, possibly against the day when I might be named Father General of the Jesuits. There were other things too, underwear and such, none of which I ever thought about—or saw—again. It was the full extent of my trousseau; nothing further was ever assessed or asked in specie or kind for my upkeep for as long as I was a Jesuit. I was giving myself, and I suppose that was enough.

We shared a couple of cabs from the Poughkeepsie train station to the Novitiate near Hyde Park and pressed an extravagant tip and all our remaining cigarettes on the drivers. They deposited us directly in front of the towering Georgian façade of our new home and disappeared back down the curving driveway toward U.S. 1. Before us was the large oaken front door of St. Andrew on Hudson, and directly behind us a statue of the Sacred Heart looked dubiously at His new recruits. Behind Him were lawns, paths and woods that slipped down to the

Hudson, which glided silently back to New York City in the July sunlight.

The nine of us were not even Novices. We were the lowest of the low, Candidates for the Novitiate, and so we were briefly greeted by the Master of Novices, an encounter that meant nothing at the time, and committed directly to the care of five real Novices, our "Angels," who introduced themselves as "Brother," a new Jesuit term to all of us. Brother David Crowe was in charge—someone was always in charge—and he was assisted by Brothers Frank Crowley, Carmody, Colombo and Scally, all of them Novices entering their second year. Their task was to walk us through the Novices' life at an easy and unfrightening pace, to break us in to the tougher but panted-after reality that lay within the cloister.

We took our little dance lessons at the "Front Door," the public rooms across the front of the building where Externs might resort. Two of those rooms were converted into a miniature Novitiate, one into a kind of study hall and the other a small dormitory. We ate in the guests' dining room, though well sequestered from the real guests, whom I already regarded with a kind of condescension as mere Externs. We kept our worldly trousers and shirts but wore vaguely clerical black jackets still worn in the gray version by some grocery clerks.

It was a skillful performance all round. The Angels were affable and relaxed, as well they might have been since I later discovered that "angeling" was one of the cushier assignments in the Novitiate. They were nicely chosen. David Crowe was superior stuff, noticeably pious without being overwhelming; very calm and very reassuring. Frank Crowley and Scally were our delegates from the "OK guy" category, marvelous companions who convinced us by their simple existence in this place that the familiar classes of being had not been annihilated. Colombo was sober and circumspect; steady or, better— the word was already emerging in Angel conversation as the ultimate compliment—*solid.* There was a hidden social message concealed there as well, but it was too early for me to detect it. Carmody was our first eccentric, a flake in the grand tradition, and I later surmised that the Master of Novices had chosen him to be an Angel as part of some personal reclamation project. A year later I found myself hoping, in vain, that even if I couldn't play the Frank Crowley part, I might still slip into next summer's angelic cast as that season's Thomas Carmody.

We prayed a little in the morning, went to Mass, cleaned our quarters, and then David Crowe gave us a brief and exceedingly unrevealing conference on the Rules, whatever they might be. After lunch we went on walks together or played whatever games our numbers permitted. All the Angels could play passably well, but Brother Colombo was just inept enough to convince Candidate LaBella that he could get through this. And perhaps it was then that Steve Toland, who abhorred sports, decided that he could *not* get through this. Jocks could smell jocks, even in our mild cavorting. Frank Crowley and Scally mentally embraced Gorman and myself, and made an urgent private note to keep an eye on Candidate Gilligan, who had World Class Competitor written all over him.

It was a pleasant, almost jolly life and it lasted two

weeks. By then I had gotten over smoking. There were simply no cigarettes available. We were informed that Jesuits could and did smoke, which I knew, but only with the permission of their Superior. I presumed that at some point, though not for four or maybe seven years, the permission would be automatic. The silence while working did not seem very difficult, and there were few other real privations. It was a little like going to camp, we all said. I had never been to camp and I'm not sure any of the others had, either.

It was not *exactly* like camp, however, even our imagined version. We were introduced enigmatically to the "Rule of Touch"—Don't. None of us particularly wanted to touch the other, but it never occurred to us that we *shouldn't*. No one dared ask why, but minds were doubtless turning. In my first year in high school, a very small Jesuit priest, who was for his sins assigned to teach a state-mandated hygiene course to us unhygienic savages, one day entered the classroom, deliberately placed his breviary on the desk before him, cleared his throat and shouted in a whisper, "Boys, if there are any problems about taking a bath, see me in private." Problems about taking a bath? That single sentence was our entire sex education, and the effect was electric. Forty adolescent minds promptly descended into the bathtub and found there in the tepid water the problem that Father Zema had so thoughtfully pointed out. The Candidates too knew with that same adolescent instinct that there would be a *lot* more to this. The Rule of Touch was filed for future reference.

If the full import of the Rule of Touch was a present

mystery, two other revelations had more substance. Brother Crowe must have rehearsed this one a thousand times. "Many religious orders have penitential practices . . . of the flesh. . . . [Oh?] The Jesuit vocation, however, demands the more difficult denial of the spirit. [Oh.] Nevertheless . . . [it was coming, whatever it was] obedience is really the highest and most rewarding of the virtues . . . [will he make it?] . . ." Suddenly they were out on the desktop before him, a foot-long whip of braided white cords and some kind of contrivance of thin chains. My spirit screamed inwardly with delight. Now *this* was more like it!

What Brother David Crowe was attempting to and finally did explain was that Jesuit Novices flagellated themselves every Monday and Wednesday night, holidays excepted. After the lights went out in the dormitory, each Novice knelt stripped to the waist at the side of his bed and at the sound of a small bell flogged himself for the space of an Our Father. It was, in my experience at least, difficult to flog yourself, to inflict pain willingly in this fashion. The chain was another matter entirely. It was kept, like the flagellum, rolled in a ball beneath the pillow. On Tuesday and Thursday mornings its inch-and-a-half width was wrapped around the thigh (my left-handed instinct told me it should be the right thigh) with its tiny wire prongs pressed inward against the flesh. Once you fixed it around your leg, there it remained until you next returned to the dormitory after breakfast, three hours hence.

The chain required considerable experimentation. If worn too loose, it would simply slip down the leg like an ungartered stocking, and the loss of face was incalculable. If bound too tightly, you saved face but possibly lost a leg. The somewhat blunted prongs were supposed to press into the flesh just enough to hurt but not to pierce. It was obviously impossible to compare tensions, torques and pain thresholds; I was reduced to checking out, as inconspicuously as I could, the red tracks on the others' thighs when next we went swimming. The really tricky part was moving. The chain was put on while standing still, but once you started walking the thigh muscles came into play and it was an entirely new deal. And in spades for genuflection. And doubled, redoubled and vulnerable when sitting down, since you sat right on the goddam chain.

We adapted. I learned to walk in a different but not a very *noticeably* different way that had a lot to do with pivoting on the ball of the foot. But we had to sit during parts of Mass and all of breakfast. And in that part lay the beauty. On those same Tuesday and Thursday mornings we were served not breakfast but a glimpse of the Beatific Vision in the form of cornbread and maple syrup. For New Yorkers who thought that God had invented breakfast simply to finish up the Wheaties, hot cornbread slathered with butter and maple syrup was like a foretaste of Paradise, the righteous's reward for celibacy. It was our sex and our dope, and of course it was put before us on the two mornings when we had to eat it sitting on steel prongs. It was the chain that yielded. Cornbread taught me that *any* pain could be borne if only the motive were strong enough.

I doubt if any Candidate ever made for the door at the

stunning revelation that he would be expected to afflict himself in this manner for the rest of his life. Like the proto-Jesuits we already were, we smiled the flagellum and the chain back into perspective. "Just what I've been looking for, a religious order that prescribes self-abuse twice a week." What was infinitely more difficult about the Candidacy was being on the outside looking in. We could see the Novices on other parts of the grounds playing their own games, and from the visitors' gallery in the upper rear of the chapel we could look down during Mass and see the entire two-hundred-man Jesuit community spread out below us. We had come to join them, and here we knelt in funny little black coats.

In the inscrutable Jesuit way we were not told how long the Candidacy would last. When Habit Day came we did not know it until after breakfast, when we returned to our dormitory to make our beds. There they were, a newly dry-cleaned black soutane, with a black cloth cincture to hold the buttonless front together, a celluloid clerical collar to be worn under the cassock, our black trousers and shoes carried with us from the World. Now dressed like Jesuits and not Externs, we were led in silence *inside* the cloister, down a dark hall we had never seen and into the basement where in a large unadorned room the Novices were waiting to greet us.

It was not exactly a meeting with strangers. There were people who had been a year ahead of me in high school to provide a social cushion. Carmody, Colombo, and Scally had all gone to Regis, and now there were others. And the Novices, it turned out, had been inspecting us even more closely than we had been marking them. We were, after all, their entertainment and fodder for the entire next year and, as they realized better than we, their companions and friends for the rest of their lives. Silent judgments had already been made, some of them based on tales carried between the two groups by the Angels, others on appearances alone. We had invested each other with an entire personal history before a single word was spoken.

We nine took our places in Novitiate life, and the Angels resumed their position to greet the next group of Candidates on August 14. A third group arrived in the first week of September and our number was then complete, thirty-six new Scholastic Novices about to embark on a fifteen-year training program. How many would survive? I have never seen statistics, but I later evolved my own. Out of every ten Candidates I estimated that two would leave during the two-year Novitiate and two more during the next eleven years prior to ordination. So sixty percent would make it to the priesthood and thereafter the fallout would be minimal. Once upon a time.

The mysteries of St. Andrew on Hudson and its inhabitants were slowly revealed in the next weeks. There were really four quite separate communities living in that house. The Fathers, as we simply referred to them, were Jesuits who had completed their training and had been ordained priests. Most were assigned there for obvious reasons, to run the house and to train the young men who had been sent there. But there were four or five Fathers who were just there. They seemed to do nothing but say Mass (some not even that), to appear at meals (sometimes) and take an occasional walk. I assumed that some were in ill health, though none had any visible malady, and that others performed tasks that were simply beyond my ken. That they might be alcoholics, victims of nervous breakdowns or dysfunctional burned-out cases occurred to no one.

The Lay Brothers, or, more technically, Coadjutor Brothers, were also Jesuits and, as it was often pointed out to us, Jesuits in the full sense. They had not entered the Society of Jesus to become priests. They took vows like everyone else, but not Holy Orders. After *their* two-year Novitiate they passed directly to the work they would be doing for the rest of their lives. At St. Andrew that work was essentially physical, running everything from the sacristy to the boiler room and the chicken farm. At other Jesuit institutions they were sometimes purchasing agents, treasurers, bookkeepers and librarians as well. But they had no say in the governance of the Jesuits, and in a society so given over to intellectual activities the Brothers must have had considerable problems of self-identity, to say nothing of self-esteem.

The remainder were Scholastics, students like me who were in training for the priesthood and final vows. This training was "the course" whose six stages covered fifteen years from where I now stood. The Novitiate lasted two years, followed by two years of Juniorate, or classical and humane studies, in this same house. You were sent elsewhere for three years of Philosophy. The next stage was called the Regency, when the Scholastic was sent to a Jesuit school, normally a high school, to teach for three years. Four years of Theology followed, with ordination to the priesthood between the third and fourth years. Last came Tertianship, so called because it was a third year of Novitiate. At its end final vows were taken.

The Scholastics in one stage of the course rarely came into contact with those in another. While normally conducted in different houses, here at St. Andrew two stages ran in parallel, though they were severely segregated. Novices and Juniors had no intercourse save in carefully staged "reunions" that took place twice a year and lasted about an hour. Rather, they lived and worked in two different wings of the same building, sat on opposite sides of the community dining room and knelt on opposite sides of the chapel.

So Fathers, Brothers, Juniors and Novices all dwelled together in this harmonious, if narrow, universe where no planet ever collided with, or even addressed, another. The entire kingdom was ruled, as was every Jesuit house, by a Father Rector, who was assisted, particularly in operational and material affairs, by someone called the Minister. The Rector governed the house, but the Novices were governed—how wretchedly inadequate the word—by the Master of Novices. The Novitiate was sacred, extraterritorial turf—"Let no one," quoth the Rule, "speak to those in their First Probation"—and the Grand Seigneur of this *haram* was the man we called, then and forever after, whatever he or we might be doing down that dim road, the Master.

The Master was the Reverend Robert Grissom, S.J. He was from Buffalo, and though at first I did not know what moral landscape lay behind that geography, it became clearer with the passing months. He was a rather short, wiry man of forty, with an outdoor complexion and a quick but somewhat forced smile that suggested that he could be amused, but neither as often nor as deeply as might first appear. His frown came almost as quickly but lasted longer, was somehow more convincing and was frequently punctuated by a vein that throbbed in quite spectacular fashion from the top of his rimless glasses to his hairline. He was not a man to be trifled with, ever.

The Master lived, like all the Fathers, in a one-room combined office and bedroom across the second-floor hallway from the large room where the Novices pondered their spiritual progress. Room 202 had a desk, a bed, a bookcase, an armoire and a prie-dieu where the Master meditated and we made our confession. There was nothing distinctive about it save its grimness, which we doubtless carried in there in our own fevered heads. It was obvious from the occasionally blue air that hung in his room and the smell of his cassock that Père Grissom smoked cigars, though never in the sight of the Novices. It was a vice beyond the admiration of eighteen-year-olds, but there was a comfort in its mere existence.

The Novices lived quite otherwise. We did not have rooms; we had two very public perches on which our lives unfolded in full view of our fellows. One was in the ominously named "ascetory," which would have been a study hall had we anything to study, and which was in fact two large connected rooms running the length and width of the second floor of the Novices' wing. Each Novice had a desk there, or rather a wooden table, with a straight-backed wooden chair and, at the right of the chair, a two-inch-high wooden kneeler. There was a shelf along one side of the table to hold our meager reading, and the table drawer contained all our earthly goods, a few pencils, a notebook or two to write down our thoughts and an eraser to erase them. Each of us also had a missal or prayerbook that he had brought with him and so was not standard issue. On almost the very first family visit each of us contrived to exchange the déclassé English-language missal of our entry for the elegantly Latin *Missale Romanum*.

On the fourth floor were two identical rooms, now divided into sleeping alcoves by suspended metal piping from which hung thin curtains. These were drawn closed only when changing or sleeping. At the far end of this floor was a washroom with rows of sinks, each with a very bad mirror and a shelf for toiletries. Sinks, beds and ascetory desks were reassigned every couple of months, and though the object of the exercise was to train us in the fine art of detachment, the effect of even that simple change in the lithic universe was as stimulating as the arrival of a shipment of prostitutes.

It would have been difficult becoming attached to those sinks in any event, since they produced nothing but cold water, *very* cold water, and for four years I began each day by shaving in that frigid stream. The johns were in a room off the main hallway on the fourth floor. There were johns in the basement as well, along with showers. The true Athlete of God took a morning shower, which demanded the preternatural effort of bolting from bed, seizing your clothes, dashing down four flights with all due modesty, and plunging your body under tepid water.

Within a half hour of rising we were expected to be present in chapel, shower or no.

The reverse trek upward at 10 P.M. unfolded with far less élan. Every day was bone-wearying in the Novitiate and a four-flight climb at its end was tolerable, as were most things in the Novitiate, only by its absolute lack of alternative. The Novice dug into his laundry box in the hall for his next day's change of shorts, socks and T-shirt, if there was such, and deposited them on the wooden chair next to his bed. There was a reluctant nod in the direction of the cold-water sink, then the silence was shattered by curtains being drawn around each bed, enclosing chair, bed and rapidly expiring Novice. The cassock was hung from the piping on a too frail wire hanger. The Novice changed from underwear to pajamas. Twice a week he awaited the sound of the Manuductor's bell to signal *flagellatio,* but otherwise he uttered some private prayer, carefully took the chain from under his pillow and placed it on the chair and sank onto his cot, a steel frame with metal straps instead of springs. The mattress was straw-filled. None of it mattered at all. There were no insomniacs in the Novices' dormitory.

Novitiate life was just becoming familiar when I was overwhelmed by a new reality, one which still towers over anything I experienced before or since. The new Novices of the first year were suddenly separated from those of the second and plunged into something that had been darkly alluded to but never really explained—the Long Retreat. Every Jesuit of whatever grade or category had to make an annual retreat, an eight-day period of intensive prayer in total silence and withdrawal from one's normal occupations and preoccupations. But twice in his training, at the very beginning and the very end, he was required to spend an entire month in such an exercise.

Ignatius of Loyola, the sixteenth-century Spanish founder of the Jesuits, had himself devised the Spiritual Exercises whose full form we were about to pursue, and he left elaborate instructions on how they were to be carried out. The retreatant is conducted by a spiritual guide through an intensive series of meditations and reflections running parallel to the life of Jesus. The conscience was to be examined, choices were to be made, resolutions formed. The Spiritual Exercises were intended, without pretense or dissembling, to change a life.

On the first day of October the first-year Novices were moved into one ascetory and one dormitory, and we began. At the end of the second day at the very latest it was already apparent to me that this was going to be a *very* long haul. Two essential changes took place: recreation disappeared and we were to meditate four times a day. It does not seem like a very radical change, given the basic premises of Novitiate life, but in fact it was.

Jesuit silence was never total; you could always ask someone to pass the salt or where the dust mops were kept. But recreation was communication, the only exit out of your own mind. We were now in effect incommunicado, sealed within ourselves and set down on our knees to think about it. Work went on as before. We sat and ate in the refectory with the same people, but all the lines were down; we were neither sending nor receiving. No hermit was ever more solitary.

Four times a day the Master presented, straight out of Saint Ignatius, the matter for meditation, and we trudged back to the ascetory, sank to our knees on those unyielding wooden kneelers and reflected upon it. I am not sure I had spent four consecutive minutes of my life reflecting about anything, and now I was being asked to spend four hours every day for a month braiding the life of Jesus and that of His newest recruit into a seamless skein of thought. From the outset I could not believe it was possible. It probably wasn't, but we all did it.

The matter for meditation was neither new nor startling; I had heard it all before in catechism classes, in sermons, novenas and what I naively thought were retreats in high school. No mysteries were revealed to a new clerical elect. The Spiritual Exercises had in fact nothing to do with the Jesuits or the priesthood. They were intended to make over an ordinary Catholic, a Christian, into a totally dedicated follower of Christ. They begged for, they demanded nothing short of a second, spiritual baptism, a conversion. You either faced it or you turned away.

Did I face it? By hindsight logic I turned away: if I had been converted in truth, I would still be a Jesuit. It did not seem that way then and it does not now. I reaffirmed my desire and determination to remain a Jesuit, but that was hardly conversion by anyone's standard, even my own. I had no new insights into either myself or the Jesuit life, and I possessed little equipment or help to attempt the first and little evidence to illuminate the latter.

Upon reflection, I am now inclined to be less kind to the Spiritual Exercises than to the very young man who was undergoing them. The Exercises were not likely designed with an eighteen-year-old from the Bronx in mind—Ignatius could not have fancied fishing in such shallow waters. I knew very little about myself, and no degree of sanctifying grace could bring visions of spiritual grandeur to my child's head and heart. I could possibly have been made to *understand,* but not by a Master of Novices who refrained from individual counsel nor by peers sealed into the same impenetrable silence as myself.

Silence seemed so natural then. It and its attendant isolation were part of the fabric of our Novitiate lives, and it seemed to follow that we should go through this solemn month in the deepest silence possible. I am no longer so certain. The Long Retreat cried out not so much for silence as for dialectic; and not with the Master of Novices, who was too obviously our ruler and our judge to join us in any genuine spiritual conversation, but among the Novices themselves. Later it would be impossible, but there at the beginning of our Jesuit lives, before the total moralization of observance took place and rendered each of us mute, we should have communed not merely with the Holy Spirit but with one another.

After it was over, we talked a great deal about the Long Retreat, but in the only way we ever discussed anything, in a distant, humorous or abstract vein. Even then we never explored what it was really like, how we fared in that cruel month, what we felt, how we were moved.

I fared poorly. I grew more restless and distracted with each passing day. I could not bear the empty solitude with myself. I counted minutes and hours and days. I thought a great deal—how could I not?—about what I cannot even recall. But I felt nothing but the desire to end that dreadful suspended animation and throw myself once again into the comforting arms of process, of life. Then, as abruptly as it had begun, the Long Retreat was over. "The Life" had now begun.

II

Regular Order

The Novitiate was entirely automated. It was run by a cybernetic device known as the Regular Order. The Master of Novices was a kind of systems engineer who checked the numbers once in a while, read out the passengers' temperatures and made a few minor adjustments. It is conceivable that he could have propped up his silhouette in the cab door of Room 202, coughed occasionally on tape and absented himself for two years without the train either stopping or derailing.

His actual silhouette was a Novice called the Manuductor who operated the Novitiate by adhering literally and eternally to a mysterious manual referred to as "the Diary." The Diary presumably recorded—no one of us had ever seen it—every Jesuit daily order back to the days of Saint Ignatius and so, like the Talmud, was tradition grown sacred in the use. And like a good Talmudist, the Manuductor had the Regular Order in his bones.

The Manuductor—the Latin word meant either "leader of the band," or "leader by the hand," and it was acceptable conversation to meditate these two meanings, though without lapsing into either cynicism or irony, an improbable task—was appointed by the Master from among the second-year Novices. A Manuductor might serve for an entire year or somewhat inexplicably be replaced in February. This latter was *never* to be interpreted as a reflection on the replaced Novice but merely as part of the Master's Inscrutable Plan. Whatever else it might have been, the possibility of a February switch in Manuductors was as wildly exciting as a change in sinks.

The choice of Manuductor was simply announced, usually at one of the Master's conferences. There was no encomium of the departing paladin, no underlining of the virtues of the Elect. No need; his virtues were usually transparent enough. First, he was almost always from Buffalo. The Master knew intuitively that the eighty percent of the Novitiate population from New York City were by and large untrustworthy. The Buffalonians, on the other hand, were the Caliph's Turks, observant, loyal and pious, qualities that only rarely emerged from the halls of Xavier High School or Brooklyn Prep and never in human memory from Regis. And yet the Master never went for the Big Bang: the *most* pious and observant Novice had as little chance of becoming Manuductor as the most worldly. It was a source of some satisfaction to me to observe that the Master could not play his highest card on the operational level. When it came to actually running things, something else had to be factored in: prudence, if you liked the current Aristotelian categories;

intelligence and common sense, as a matter of cold fact.

When I took up sackcloth and ashes and cornbread for breakfast, the Manuductor was Brother Heilig, a prime example of the species. He was a blond, bland Buffalonian who managed to be observant of the Rules without displaying either freakishness or fanaticism. There were residual signs of a sense of humor, though it was kept, like the Master's own, under careful and humorless control; he had, in short, an *appropriate* sense of humor. He was, as the Novices piously intoned, *solid,* a pillar of the Novitiate community whom you could safely ignore for the rest of your Jesuit life.

Except that no one ever ignored *his* Manuductor. Every eighteen-year-old entering Novice was bonded like an orphaned gosling to the nineteen-year-old who was his first Manuductor. Years later I found myself staring at Mr. Heilig and Father Heilig with that careful and curious gaze reserved for the Manuductor. He was, and remained, that simple frozen youth, something mysterious and special.

The Manuductor had no particular powers over the Novices. He was as much a servant of the Regular Order as the rest of us, and he had about as much authority to alter it as a Muslim to rewrite the Koran. He had few patronage items to dispense and certainly no wickedness to visit upon his enemies. By definition he had no enemies; he was above such pettiness, or else he would not have been Manuductor. Perhaps he was intended to be a role model; for most of us he was just Different.

It was probably his prolonged and intimate contact with the Master of Novices that rendered the Manuductor taboo. Most Novices entered the private presence of the Master only when summoned, and that was *never* for a benign purpose ("Brother, you're working too hard. Why don't you go down to New York for a weekend, see a couple of movies and relax"). The Manuductor, on the other hand, like some High Priest of Election, parted the curtains and entered the Holy of Holies as part of his regular duties. One could only dimly imagine what *that* was like, what relaxed and pleasant little chitchat went on in Room 202 on those occasions. It was a transparent fallacy, of course: the Master was Master and the Manuductor was Manuductor precisely because they did not indulge in idle chitchat.

Most of the Manuductor's duties were perfectly visible. He sat in the rear of the ascetory near the door, from which post he was readily available both to the Master across the hall outside (the Master only very rarely came into the ascetory himself) and to the bulletin board behind him on which the daily order was posted. He made all the work assignments on the basis of what seemed to be a satisfactorily rotating order. He assigned bands at recreation. He kept the Diary. He led common prayers. And he set good example everywhere and at all times. It must have been an exhausting job.

He had an assistant called the Sub-Manuductor, always called the Sub, except by the Master, who called him Brother Sub-Manuductor. The Novice Sub was a kind of quartermaster: he took care of things and events, like shoe repairs and outings. It was not a bad job, since it possessed the possibility of both escaping the Regular Order and dispensing patronage. Best of all, the Sub was not bound in the kind of eternal thralldom to Good Example that defined the role of the Manuductor. The Master's choices for the office reflected the job. New Yorkers and jocks could and did become Subs, even some with that *look* in their eye, provided of course that they were *solid*. It was a delicate nuance and the Master navigated it with virtuoso skill.

There were other Novice officials: a Sub-Sub-Manuductor who was inevitably and condescendingly a "good guy" and whose duties were so microscopic that it was generally thought that he served only in the unlikely cases of (1) a worldwide shoe repair epidemic or (2) the sudden death of a Sub-Manuductor. A Novice Brother Sacristan worked the many chapels in the house in some mysterious and so satisfying way, and, more, he labored under one of the Lay Brothers, Brother Walzer, who was the real Sacristan. That too was presumed to be interesting, even though Brother Walzer appeared to spend most of his time entertaining himself by playing the chapel organ in an outlandish stop known as "vox humana." Each of these viziers and notaries carried a visible sign of office, not peacock feathers but a large Ingersoll watch suspended around the neck on a black shoelace. These were normally tucked into the inside breast pocket of the cassock. Exposed, they shone like the Star of India.

The Manuductor posted the next day's order of activities in the ascetory on the way to bed. It glowed there under a single bulb in the darkened room like a theatrically illumined Dead Sea Scroll. It was tomorrow, our tomorrow, and whatever happened then would occur around and between its terse lines. When a new group of

Novices entered, the daily order was spelled out in some detail:

> 1–1:45: *Recreatio vel Mandata*
> 2:00–2:15: *Preces*
> 2:30–2:45: *Lectio spiritualis* [etc.]

The detail was misleading. The daily order was in fact extremely detailed, but there was no need of spelling it out. Every one of us had it by heart, and eventually the *lectio plenior* was replaced by the numbing reality:

Feria Tertia: Ordo Regularis

That was it and all of it. "Tuesday: Regular Order," the Novices' routine that stretched back to the Age of the Patriarchs and would presumably continue even unto those Novices who entered the Jesuits just this side of the Crack of Doom.

The order was indeed regular, but it was also *regularis,* prescribed by the Rule. Devotion to the *sacra regula* was a very old tradition in the religious life, and the rules of some monastic orders spelled things out in elaborate detail. The Jesuit Rules were in fact very few and ranged from the very general (avoid worldliness) to an elegant Latin imprecation that all, *etiam si sacerdotes sint*—even if they be priests—should make their beds in the morning.

The Regular Order was not, then, Rule, but Tradition, some of it a century old and some a hoary week and a half, for all we knew. This is the purest hindsight: no one ever contested the daily order. In their folly the first-year

Novices prayed that tomorrow perhaps tradition would dictate an entire morning of sports followed by a long nap, a table-staggering feast at dinner and a movie to cap off the evening. Their seniors knew better: one had simply to look down the calendar of the ecclesiastical year, identify every single holiday, measure its specific liturgical gravity and draw the appropriate conclusions as to the likelihood of a softball game after lunch or a fruit cocktail before dinner.

In deep, rock-bottom, bone-crushing Regular Order we rose at five-thirty, got our bodies, if not always our minds, to the chapel by six for silent prayer together. At the stroke of six—at St. Andrew chapel bells tolled every fifteen minutes—we went to the ascetory for an hour's meditation. Mass at seven, breakfast at eight. As each finished breakfast he went back to the dormitory, made his bed (and removed his chain, if that seemed like a good idea) and put on work clothes. Then began the morning's work: cleaning up after breakfast and setting up for lunch; or helping prepare lunch and dinner in the kitchen beneath the refectory; or general cleaning around the huge house.

At eleven there was a conference by the Master of Novices, followed by some free time, a fifteen-minute examination of conscience, and lunch. After lunch some had cleanup and the rest had recreation for about forty-five minutes, outdoors in tolerable weather, indoors in foul. Then came "Prayers" in chapel, spiritual reading, more work, the afternoon's half-hour meditation, dinner, an hour recreation period, more spiritual reading, a sliver of free time, preparation of the morrow's meditation, community litanies, another examination of conscience, a final visit to the chapel, and lights out at 10 P.M.

Time did not pass; it stumbled by in pieces of varying sizes, each marked by the ringing of a bell. It was a life devoid of leisure: we did not relax, we recreated; we did not read, we had an assigned time for "spiritual reading," like the fifteen minutes given over every Saturday to the leaden pieties of Thomas à Kempis' *Imitation of Christ,* which cruelly advised us, "Be rarely with young people and strangers." There was even an assigned time for social improvement, fifteen Sunday minutes of something called *scriptio,* when we were adjured to improve our handwriting. When we were all older and wiser, it was widely speculated that *scriptio* had been introduced for the benefit of Maryland Jesuits, most of whom were illiterate.

Almost everything the Novices did, we did in concert. The work duties were spread around and changed every week or so, but for the rest we moved like a large black centipede between dormitory, ascetory, refectory and chapel, always in single file along the wall at the right hand. The system delivered bodies in an efficient and quiet manner, but it also focused an inordinate amount of attention on the gait and carriage of the person immediately ahead. It was also carried out in silence: the only time conversation was permitted was at dinner on Thursday and Sunday and during the recreation periods after lunch and dinner.

As the Long Retreat had taught me, recreation was an event of great magnitude. Nothing was carried out in absolute silence, of course. Brief talk was permitted when absolutely necessary, and the fertile Novice mind discovered more necessity in the world than a deranged Stoic in a lifetime. But these were not real conversations, and they had, moreover, to be conducted in Latin, which was inhibiting, to say the least. So true communication, the analysis of the day's events, the evaluation of motives, simple gossip, and the all-important prognosis of what tomorrow might bring, all had to await recreation. We had to make some sense of what was happening to us, to sort the sense from the nonsense in a world which now appeared to be completely sensible and now the very attar of nonsense, and for this we all needed counsel, another perspective, an audience for a large pinch of soul-saving humor and a metaphorical shoulder for our equally metaphorical tears.

That is what recreation was about. What it was *for* was to provide us with an opportunity to exercise charity. So outside the back door of the Novices' wing the Manuductor assembled the brethren afternoon and evening for another essay at charity. It was he who proclaimed the opening of recreation with a Latin piety, and those who were involved in cleanup and so joined recreation in progress had to pursue the Manuductor in silence until they too could be touched by his Latin magic and lapse miraculously into speech.

The Manuductor's first move at recreation was to dispatch some willy-nilly "bands," groups of three, a second-year and two first-year Novices, to recreate together. As these disconsolate trios disappeared into the gloaming, the Manuductor and the survivors of this terrible triage moved slowly and noisily down the paths and lawns of St. Andrew toward the river. There in a large rustic gazebo overlooking the Hudson we all learned to talk very rapidly indeed because sooner or later the Manuductor's finely attuned biological clock would go off and he and his cortege would ascend the same paths to arrive at the back door precisely as the chapel bell tolled 8 P.M. and the end of recreation. The assigned bands were frequently there before the Manuductor, bloodily battered by their encounter with charity.

Bands were not always assigned; just as often there were "free bands," when a senior Novice presented himself to the Manuductor and announced the names of two other more junior Novices with whom he wished to stroll off. This quasi-request was never denied, but it was clearly understood that one should "mix" at recreation, and going off incessantly or even remarkably with one's friends was not an acceptable form of "mixing," even in Jesuit Patagonia. The Manuductor assigned bands to enrich the mix; the pious used assigned bands to seize two neophytes and shoot them mischievously through with charity until they looked and felt like Saint Sebastian.

Recreation was a tricky business in the Novitiate. It could be depressing, particularly in the company of a brace of cretins in an assigned band lurching eyelessly through a dark winter night toward the frozen Hudson. This was one of my two chances to say anything coherent in any given day, and to spend it listening to Brother Looney dither on about the beauties of the liturgy required patience and the firm conviction that I would live to see recreation on the morrow. But forty-five minutes with Brother Brennan or Brother Flynn banished devils and restored the spirit.

The best conversations in that society were on the taboo subject of "personalities." We might presumably discuss the fact that Brother Heilig was the Manuductor or that Father Hubbard was "the Glacier Priest," but to suggest that the former was possibly a dolt and the latter likely a charlatan was completely regrettable, totally absorbing and thoroughly entertaining. In his conferences the Master tried desperately to lay out some of the acceptable topics of Novice conversation, like "the virtues of Ours, particularly the dead," but it was quite obviously a lost cause. Cut off from books, news and ideas, we had only ourselves and our microscopic range of activities to pick over. How to praise the Holy Father when we were not even sure who was the Holy Father, much less what he was currently up to? We had only the slenderest idea of even Jesuit history, and so we wallowed in contemporary biography, our own. Or we explored, for our own amusement and instruction, the intricacies of "The Life," or at least that tiny fragment of it exposed to our view.

I and the other proto-Jesuits who arrived at the Novitiate had seen the daily order before. It coursed through the arteries of Jesuit high schools, though in that setting it had no particular religious significance. There it was The Game, rules to be evaded or outwitted in the most elegant way possible, where one could produce the desired effect with only lip service to the means. The Jesuit educational system rewarded verbal and literary precocity and the powers of quick absorption and recognition; it taught us to distinguish with brilliance and rationalize with aplomb. It liked its young academic scholars slick and sassy.

It was many of those same achievers who reported to St. Andrew on Hudson to discover that The Game was now The Life, a system as richly and invitingly complex as the one they had just left. For me the issue of the Novitiate life was not the classic struggle that was fought on the ground of the vows but the contest between the mordant and mocking spirit of the Jesuit-trained and the officially simple-minded acceptance of the Jesuit trainee, between high religious seriousness and amused detachment. Rich veins of irony grew even richer within those grave halls, but there was an interior point at which the publicly expressed cynicism had to end and acceptance prevail. Regular Order could be and was treated as an adversary by many Novices in an easy, familiar and even affectionate fashion. But if The Life was *only* an adversary, then one's Jesuit days were clearly self-numbered.

None of us had come to that place as intellectuals. All presumably knew how to read, however, and what we were given to practice on was an entirely new genre, even now neglected by most literary critics, "spiritual reading." There were some treatments of Jesuit saints, hagiography rather than biography, which could strain the credulity even of an eighteen-year-old. The most common form of reading, however, was a kind of "Guide to the Spiritual Life," and the archetype of the genre was written by one Alphonsus Rodríguez, S.J., a Spanish Jesuit of an indeterminate era, perhaps the Late Bronze, and was read to us aloud in season and out while we worked and was strongly recommended for private spiritual reading as well.

Rodríguez threw his spiritual meringue straight from the shoulder, and it was an easy enough matter to tune out as the pious platitudes drifted through the din of dishwashing. But he erred grievously. After every couple of hundred slices of Velveeta, Rodríguez introduced a chapter entitled "Whereby the Preceding Is Confirmed by Example." His examples all harked back to an earlier, raunchier era of spirituality, to the Fathers of the Egyptian desert mostly, when monks were monks and were beset by temptations that were both exceedingly graphic and transparently paranoid.

My earlier Catholic education had quietly, and wisely, passed over the Desert Fathers, those half-mad Copts who fled the fleshpots of fourth-century Alexandria in search of salvation in the Wadi Natrun. Was there really a Blessed Macarius who found piety in plaiting wicker baskets and endlessly genuflecting? And a Blessed Shenoute who could do both simultaneously? Saint Simon Stylites lived forty years atop a pillar, but only after preparing himself by spending the two previous decades standing in a hole. What these Jim Thorpes of perverse asceticism were intended to mean to us was beyond even the most pious or bizarre speculation. But they certainly had our attention, especially the passage where a notorious monastic backslider—he wanted curtains in his cell— met his end by having his bowels explode in a public latrine.

The reaction to Rodríguez' little desert vignettes was as

predictable as Regular Order itself. When a very observant Novice was in charge of the work crew, and so of its
reader as well, he would simply bid "that part" be passed
over in the public reading. The brave, the bold or the
foolhardy skipped over as many of the intervening
chapters as they dared and dove headlong into "The
Preceding Confirmed . . ." to entertain the keelers of
greasy pots and the scrubbers of egg-encrusted plates.
What each did in his own private reading of Padre
Rodríguez was a matter, as the Master loved to say of
other, more fatal choices, between himself and God.
Surmise had a ready answer, however.

The Regular Order prevailed every day except Thursdays and Sundays and on special feast days of the Church
and the Society of Jesus. The Feast of the Immaculate
Conception I already knew about, since it was celebrated
as a holiday even in remote Catholic enclaves in the
Bronx. But here I discovered exotic new heroes like the
Blessed Claude de la Colombière, S.J., whose involve-
ment with Titus Oates and the Gunpowder Plot was thin
enough to warrant only a Double of the Second Class in
the Church's labyrinthine hierarchy of holydays, but a
feast day nonetheless, and the undoubtedly First Class
North American Martyrs, whose cult held other, later
surprises for me.

Both Church and Society failed us in January, February
and March, the doleful "tunnel months" of Novitiate
myth. Martyrdom appears to have been rare in the
winter, nor were the astrological signs favorable to even
that kind of middling holiness that produced a Double
Second Class and so a softball game. It was Lent and we

were on our own in a bad time. The Hudson froze over and icy fingers grew tight around the throat of Brother Walzer's *vox humana* in the organ. The dormitories became the silent but grim battleground for the fanciers of fresh air—from Buffalo, *bien sûr*—and those softer creatures who had become accustomed to life after dark.

It was not dark at 5:30 A.M.; it was impenetrable, and there was only the sound of icily splashing water in the washrooms to guide my frozen limbs from bed to sink. A cup of coffee was still two and a half hours away, beyond even a Novice's anticipation, and so I creaked down to the chapel, because there was no place else to go, and then to the ascetory, where the Battle of Lake Erie was resumed by the Softs and the Crazies during the morning meditation.

There were pleasant surprises in the Novitiate, as well. For the first time I felt the full impact of the Church year as it unfolded in its entirety. The mood of the liturgy changed as gradually but as perceptibly as the seasons. Christmas was a starburst in the midst of winter. There were no gifts or greetings, but the explosion of light, music and red flowers on the high altar was as glorious as a child's Noël. The warmth and the light spread out around the dark grounds, over the crusted snow, into our hearts and our very bones. Easter was earned, and so all the more precious and beautiful after a dour and silent Lent filled with purple and fasts. Easter fell like a warm spring rain on our parched souls. We all suddenly grew green and fresh, revived by a Mass.

Every Thursday was a holiday and a minor revelation in that it was really a much better place to break a week than Saturday. On Thursdays we burst out of doors, and there were marvelous new opportunities for charity on the softball field and in the woods. Sunday afternoon too was a relaxed out-of-doors time, and the ordinary work assignments were left untouched on Sunday mornings. It was almost as if the Church had created a vacuum into which some later genius had dropped *The New York Times*. But not on us Novices. We had long since forgotten there even existed such things as newspapers.

No day, not even Christmas and Easter, the blockbusters of the liturgical year (Doubles of the First Class with a Privileged Octave of the First Class), was unstructured. The Rule explicitly banned leisure from the Jesuit life (the forbidden *otium* was translated as "leisure" chiefly for the benefit of Novices; the more philologically astute Fathers preferred "idleness" and never, never confused that with "relaxation"), and the daily order on the ascetory bulletin board never read *Dies ad libitum,* "Take the day off." Instead, a holiday mandated out of the eternal wisdom of the Diary that the Novices would do this rather than that, simple in the saying, but a blessed relief from regularity. Any change, any diversion or interruption of the Regular Order, had all the aura of a Plenary Indulgence.

There was variety, however, even within the forbidding confines of the Regular Order, and you made what you could of it. A truly existential eccentric like Brother Dromgool might spend his free time memorizing the unabridged dictionary at the rear of the ascetory or endlessly scrutinizing the jejune notices on the bulletin board as if they were the words of the *I Ching*. But most took their pleasure in those little subplanetary motions, some invisible to the secular naked eye, that occurred in the great cosmic revolutions of the Regular Order, the social roulette of recreation, for example, or the weekly change in work assignments.

Novices did two kinds of work. *Mandata,* "assignments," were the cleanup details that worked in the dining room and the scullery after the noon and evening meals. *Manualia,* the more straightforward "work," took place after breakfast when we were sorted out around that great house to dust, scrub and polish for two hours in the name of Holy Obedience and a more perfect self-denial. We rotated through these tasks without demur, though each assignment doubtless had its own place in the forbidden but inevitable order of preferences tattooed onto the mind of everyone who had not perfectly adapted himself to the will of God.

The *mandata* were a very special challenge, however, since they were cut out of recreation time. Every fourth week or so you had no cleanup and so went directly to recreation after meals; otherwise you joined recreation in progress as soon as you and your crew finished its assigned task. That decision rested with the Novice in charge, and the degree of his scrupulosity was an exact inverse gauge of the temper of his charges. Brother Zweifel, who was from a *suburb* of Buffalo, really wanted every knife and fork straight on the table—as if anyone cared, commented the theological naif—while Brother Meeker managed his crew with such smart yet impeccable alacrity that they were into greatcoats and slipping and sliding toward the Hudson well before the Manuductor had exhausted his prepared supply of conversational topics.

Brother Gilligan was both loco and immoral and held that even washing the dishes was a vanity compared to recreation time. If he had believed in the Holy Spirit, he would have left the wash-up in His hands; and if they had believed in main force, the rest of his crew would have constrained him at least to breathe upon the dishes before hurling them pell-mell on the tables and rushing off to the gazebo. His cry *"Frater, noli scrupulare,"* "Brother, don't scruple," rang noisily across the refectory whenever his eagle eye detected some new Novice unused to the Gilligan method witlessly attempting to wash a dish. It was rumored to be the first, last and only Latin expression that Brother Gilligan ever mastered.

The work we were assigned to do was not particularly strenuous, nor was it very interesting. The least interesting and probably the only *terrible* task we were set to was gathering in the basement laundry room on Saturday mornings and sorting the Novices' dirty laundry for shipment to what was thought to be a convent of the Good Shepherd, the haunt of nuns who reputedly rehabilitated wayward girls by making them do the laundry of sanctified but very dirty Jesuit Novices.

We were always filthy, sometimes by inclination but often through circumstance. We each wore the same cassock day in and day out. Summer in the Hudson Valley is not a kindly season, and a dripping cassock hung up by the bed at night was still damp in the morning. Meals dribbled down our chests despite the best of intentions, and attempts at cleaning the front of the cassock, which already had previous owners when it was handed to us, inevitably turned the black serge to a vile color somewhere between green and gray. Arms and elbows became frayed and discolored from constant rubbing on desktops. We were issued four pairs of shorts, T-shirts and socks each week, all of them army surplus, which some Lay Brother had obviously bought for a chant. Everything came in one size, and though the shorts could theoretically be adjusted by little tie strings on the side, the immense or dwarfed private first class who first tied them on Okinawa in 1944 had tied them forever.

Cleanliness, it was understood, was a virtue in some remote sense that didn't really count, and it was not much pushed at St. Andrew except that you were expected to shave daily. The Master was always clean, though not too noticeably so. Some of the other Fathers clearly indulged in such worldly affectations as Mennen After-Shave, but not Robert Grissom, S.J. He preached, in the subtle gnostic fashion in which such things were done, some undefined but perfectly clear code of "manly virtue." It was not machismo—the sexual corollaries of that rendered it useless in the circumstances—but a striving to be a "real man," and, whatever that meant, it did not include foppishness or even a remarkable care of your fleshly envelope.

If we avoided foppishness by a margin that would have put a Pharisee to shame, hypochondria was a more subtle temptation of the flesh. In that life of intense self-inspection and constant striving toward an extraordinary variety of goals, the spiritual athlete might easily find an astonishing range of aches and pains that carried with them the not inconsiderable bonus of providing acceptable grounds—there were, in fact, no others—for dropping out of the race for a few hours or a few days.

Gerry Garvin, the jolly Lay Brother who ran the infirmary and learned whatever medicine he knew at the foot of a statue of the Blessed Virgin, would willingly connive at ailments because he was new at his job and so was as eager to have us as patients as we to become them, provided that no real illness was involved. But no one got to that infirmary and its blessed beds without first passing the terrible scrutiny of the Master of Novices, who was notoriously unsympathetic to anything short of a ruptured spleen and who enjoyed, in the divine order of things, a quite perfect health himself. Headaches and colds went absolutely unrewarded at his stern tribunal. We all prayed for a ruptured spleen.

It was not that the Master was unaware of the mental condition of his charges. It was piously believed that he had his hand on the collective pulse of the Novitiate and could detect the telltale signs of "tightness," a mysterious but real psychic condition that affected both individuals and groups. When the Novices were getting "tight," a hypothesis which we discussed always and everywhere in the expectation of getting some relief, it was thought that the Master made some subtle adjustment of the Regular Order and so avoided mass thrombosis. The evidence that he ever really did so was, as usual, exceedingly slight, but we prescribed and took our own placebo nonetheless. It was not good form to plead "tightness" for one's own eccentric behavior, but we all made free to attribute it to others, sometimes genuinely and sympathetically, some-times maliciously to Novices for whom "trying too hard" was so inconceivable as to be ludicrous, or to professional hairshirts who came "tight" from their mothers' womb.

"Everything is easy for those who love Christ." The phrase may have been conjured up to explain how anyone could survive something as apparently difficult as the Regular Order. "Everything is easy for an eighteen-year-old" is an equally likely explanation. I did not find the Novice's life particularly onerous, which it probably wasn't, or even extraordinary, which it certainly was. I had volunteered for this, and if it was not quite what I had anticipated, it did not come as an unbearable surprise. Most persuasively of all, it was part of a package deal: I took all of it or none of it. Unless I was willing simply to concede that I did not have a vocation to the Jesuit life, I could have no quarrel with the work, the silence and the prayer. And I had no reason to think that I did not have such a vocation.

III

The Religious Life

The chains of the Regular Order merely outlined the ground on which the great struggle to achieve the Jesuit version of sanctity unfolded. It was now time to fill in the details of what would be, after fifteen years, a finished portrait. And the first strokes were laid down in the Novitiate.

The Novitiate was an unashamedly encapsulated system: Jesuit piety and Jesuit perfection were equated with Novitiate piety, and it was understood that here in this eccentric Novitiate world, eccentric even by comparison to the other Jesuits who lived in that same house, we were acquiring virtues that would last us our entire Jesuit lives. By intent the Novitiate was constructed around those virtues in their absolute form and not on the model of the actual life that most of us would later lead as Jesuits. Once in the Novitiate, I found all recollection of former teachers, the Moores, La Baus, Cullens and other real

Jesuits of the recent past, the very men whose example led me to this place, quickly faded in the bright new glare of Novitiate piety.

We lived in a rare world. Just as Roman Catholicism seemed to have little to do with what many people called Christianity, so the Jesuits seemed to float free of the Catholic Church. Ours liked to think of themselves as the Church's elite troops, the Pope's Marine Corps. More likely they were his Pretorian Guard or Janissaries with their own traditions, their own internal loyalties and their own chain of command, a Church within a Church. No bishop had jurisdiction over the Jesuits, and they in turn showed little interest and even occasional disdain for the life and ongoing business of the Church.

I was now a Novice in the Society of Jesus, and I bore the initials N.S.J. after my name to attest to the fact. I was there because in high school at age eighteen I thought I had a vocation. I had submitted myself and my vocation to the test of the Long Retreat at whose climactic moment, called "The Election," I was exhorted to choose only those means that were conducive to the final end and purpose of life, namely, the salvation of my soul and the greater glory of God. This last phrase, in its Latin version, *Ad Majorem Dei Gloriam,* was in effect the motto of the Jesuits, and every Jesuit schoolboy from New York to Rome, Baghdad, Tokyo and back faithfully inscribed the initials A.M.D.G. on the top of every page he ever wrote.

I and the others in that dark ascetory had chosen the Jesuit life as our means to salvation and God's glory, not a bad choice under the circumstances, and the rest of the Novitiate was designed to convert that election into Jesuit spirituality and Jesuit behavior: the religious life, Jesuit style.

The Jesuits didn't invent the religious life, as that term is understood in the Christian tradition. It started in fourth-century Egypt when certain of the pious faithful decided that steamy Alexandria was not an ideal setting for putting on the New Man and so fled the World and its works to the desert, where they lacerated their flesh and their psyches in a quite exemplary fit of devotion. First as solitaries and then under a common roof, they embraced a voluntary poverty and celibacy with as natural an instinct as holy men have all over the world. Eventually they discovered that the will had its pleasures as well and that too went under the lash of self-denial: the religious submitted his will to that of another, who spoke to him with the voice of God.

That was only the beginning, but however primitive it sounded to us when those half-crazed Egyptians wandered across the pages of Rodríguez, all the essentials of our own Jesuit life were there: vows or promises of perpetual poverty, chastity and obedience to a religious superior and a community life governed not by personal whim but by Rule.

There were some Jesuit refinements, however. When Ignatius of Loyola gathered his first community around him in 1534, he didn't intend to create yet another order of monks. The Franciscans, Dominicans and Benedictines could pursue their version of Egyptian-style monasticism in their abbeys and convents; what Ignatius had in mind was to produce religious with the fiber, temperament and cohesiveness of the monastic communities but who would live and work in the World. The Jesuits might appear to Externs like ordinary parish priests, but under those unassuming black cassocks—nothing special in that—they would be world-class athletes of God, as tough and as tested as if they had been bred and raised in the fiery oven of Egyptian asceticism.

The Novitiate was to be our version of the Egyptian desert, where eighteen-year-olds from the Bronx, Queens and New Jersey would be formed into true *Milites Christi*, "Soldiers of Christ." There's no way you warm up for poverty, chastity and obedience, of course; you just start in. But there was help. The environment was highly controlled, and so the opportunity for amassing or enjoying large hordes of women, worldly possessions or ego gratifications was severely limited. But even the Egyptians knew that you don't become poor or chaste or obedient in that simple privative fashion. What about the phantom ladies who dance in the head and make their silent carouse in the loins? What of the extra pencil that looms so large in my desires? And, well, who's to notice if I lie here in bed for a scant two minutes after the bell bids me rise? They didn't want my body; they wanted, didn't I see, my head and my heart and my will: think poor, live chaste, love obedience.

It didn't seem very difficult to think poor. The Novitiate was much like living on a collective or in a socialist society of a particularly utopian type: necessities procured by the goodwill offerings of the faithful, the much-maligned Externs, were distributed according to the presumably identical needs of the religious. I had been a family dependent a few months earlier. Now I was a dependent in an even-handed distributive system that had neither barter nor currency and no need for either. I was fed, clothed, heated and entertained when and as required. Poverty, Jesuit-style, seemed like a snap.

Chastity was perhaps a snap and a half. The eighteen-year-olds of that time and place were hardly slaves to lubricity. In fact, the odds were good that no one among the Novices had ever experienced intercourse, and my own unnourished recollections of kissing and petting with Catholic maidens who had had their knees bolted together at birth rapidly faded into a ghostly abstraction. But they never quite disappeared, and when those pale negatives were stitched together with faint images from otherwise innocuous movies and half-forgotten conversations and fed with my considerable powers of fantasy into a softly growling unconscious, they would occasionally hurl some invisible erotic lightning bolt into my head at Mass or meditation or else would powerfully and inevitably erupt in wet dreams.

"Nocturnal emissions," as they called them, troubled the moral theologians, who really didn't much approve of sex without sin. But that is precisely what they were, God and Dr. Freud's graphic and realistically erotic rewards to the celibate. The sheets might be stained, but I was as clean as Saint Joseph riding his bike with no hands. But Saint Joseph, we were given to understand, kept his hands well off the bars while awake, and that was the hard part. The recollection of wet dreams unfortunately lingered on into the waking hours, when I *was* responsible for the contents of my head, and if that erection came and went with a rhythm apparently all its own, I was best advised to keep both head and hands off. And to help us along, the Novices were kept busy enough to discharge much of that eroticism in a subliminal cloud of distraction and softball. As a Novice I played enough softball to turn a satyr into a eunuch.

The vow of chastity provokes everything from derisive laughter to the most perfect incredulity from Externs, particularly the heathen variety, whom I am much among these days. Well, maybe. I was not privy to others' confessions or the contents of their heads. But every Catholic male from the age of seven onward was schooled, day after day, in sermon, chant and retreat, if not on the virtues of chastity, then even more persuasively on the eternally damning consequences of "impurity in thought, word and deed." The struggle against impure thoughts and masturbation was fought in every theological trench and foxhole in the Bronx. The Jesuit struggle was identical—the cloistered Jesuit and the single Extern lived by the same rules when it came to chastity—except that the Novice's motives had been strengthened and the environment considerably sanitized. Difficult, yes, but impossible it wasn't. As a matter of fact, obedience and charity were far more difficult than celibacy.

The center of the Jesuit system lay in the third of the great triad, obedience. Obedience as a virtue, a habit of mind and the will, meant following the direct commands of the Jesuit Superior, or his delegate, *perinde ac cadaver*, "much like a corpse," as the Rules delicately put it. There were, however, few such direct commands "by virtue of Holy Obedience" in the normal Jesuit life. Jesuits could be and were assigned anywhere at any time, as I would be at each new stage of the course of study, when the annual "status,"* as it was called, was posted in every Jesuit house. But when the fifteen-year training period was over, a transfer to a new position was a far more serious business and more often than not there was prior consultation between Superior and subject on the matter.

The Jesuits prided themselves on being both mobile and adaptable, as indeed they were, since the chain of command was clear-cut from subject to Superior of his house, normally the Rector, from Rector to Province Superior, from Provincial to the Father General of the entire Society of Jesus, and from the General to the Pope. Did the Pope have some new project? A memo to the Father General at No. 5, Borgo Santo Spirito, a stone's throw from the Pope's Vatican study, would start the obedient Jesuit wheels in motion, whence they would grind downward until shortly thereafter Father P. J. Moriarity, S.J., would be plucked from his soft perch at Fordham University and sent off to catechize the Aleuts or to start a new magazine called *Getting to Know the Catholic Church*.

The Jesuits had been founded precisely to give the Pope just such a supple tactical weapon against heretics within and infidels without the Church. Over the course of centuries the Order had settled into a great many routine duties that represented a considerable and ongoing investment of manpower and money and which had noticeably reduced their flexibility of response: somebody had to

---

*"Status" is the Jesuit shibboleth. All past and present Jesuit tongues are betrayed by their absolute inability to pronounce that English word in any fashion other than the Latinate "stähtus."

staff, run and raise the money for Loyola University and Creighton and Santa Clara and all the other universities and high schools that the Jesuits owned and operated across the United States. But the tradition remained, and every Jesuit Father who survived the rigors of the full course, when he repeated his three vows of poverty, chastity and obedience added a new fourth, a vow of obedience to the Pope.

It was far from an empty gesture. The Pope might not presently be much inclined to uproot large numbers of Jesuits and send them to Uganda or bid them close Holy Cross and Boston College and open a soup kitchen in Roxbury instead, but he could and did tell individual Jesuits to hold their tongues, to cease and desist from whatever dubious practices or temerarious theology they were advancing or even, as Clement XIV did in 1773, to close down the entire operation. The entire Jesuit Order was suppressed once, and the Jesuits had not forgotten. They hadn't exactly mended their ways either, but the world had changed since then and so had their own power, though the names of the villains of that particular piece, the dastardly Pombal and the insidious Choiseul, still remained embedded in Jesuit mythology.

All of these grave apostolic turnings were remote from Novices, of course; we were being trained, not sent out to do battle, Papal or otherwise. And in our case, the Master of Novices commanded nothing. His will, and indeed the collective will of the entire Society of Jesus, was expressed in our practicing the Jesuit Rules, in the letter and in the spirit. All Jesuits, Novices or not, were supposed to live by the Rule, but in our case the Rule was converted into the thousand mundane details of the daily order. If it said "8:30 P.M.: Spiritual Reading," that is what we were supposed to be doing, promptly and even lovingly.

Following the daily order was not particularly difficult, since there were no real alternatives, nor even a place to go and contemplate their absence. But when the Master spoke of "observance," he was not talking about some routine performance or going through the motions but rather of a large and generous embrace of the whole system in its every detail, that you regarded it not as an adversary to be bested but as a manifestation, no matter how many times removed, of the will of God. And that was not easy.

The Life demanded more than just the meat and potatoes of poverty, chastity and obedience; it required as well the sauce that rendered the sacrifice savory, charity. If obedience meant accepting the system, charity meant accepting the others who had chosen to embrace it at my side. And like obedience, charity was a dreadfully difficult business. I could, I suppose, despite constant provocation, resist the temptation to garrot Brother Suchard or set fire to Brother Geller's bed some evening after lights out. But what I was being asked was that I accept them, and if not with glowing affection—the Jesuits only occasionally required the improbable—then with a certain tolerant understanding.

Living in a community of seventy-five males is probably difficult under the best of circumstances and downright forbidding when the seventy-five are all eighteen- and nineteen-year-olds marching in lockstep under the transparent roof of a single greenhouse. It helps, you suppose, that material distinctions are stripped away and that we all lived clad in anonymous cassocks in bare, shared quarters. But individuality is made of sterner stuff. A cassock can be worn high or low; the varieties of genuflection are simply unimaginable; walks are as individually eccentric as fingerprints. We lived so close that we could look down one another's pores and immediately we noticed that pores are different.

No one was murdered, maimed or even struck in the Novitiate while I was there, though the temptation to bash brains was at times overwhelming. But if the fist, the refectory knife or the softball bat was never invoked, the tongue always lay ready-honed. Malicious and terrible gossip was too gross by far, and even the very dense and the very angry perceived that neither direct verbal assault nor slanderous backbiting was an acceptable way of dealing with a fellow novice. You either held your tongue or developed more delicate instruments of hostility, stilettolike thrusts that left the victim as finely filleted as a wondering flounder. Novices never confronted each other; like the Bedouin at pasture, the quarters were far too close and the system simply would not tolerate it. They sheared off, suppressed, prayed for charity or tried an occasional bank shot.

I felt more strongly about some of my fellow Novices than I publicly allowed, even to confidants. Fortunately, charity restrained our hostile impulses and stopped our too supple mouths, if not on all occasions, then often enough to enable us to deal with one another in some kind of reasonable social terms. There were no feuds, no bloody breaches of *omertà*, no pistols in the foggy dawn under the elms. We treated each other with civil good humor and with a certain degree of restraint. It was difficult, for example, to let escape, even in the most congenial and sympathetic company, the kind of primal outburst that the lamented Brother Gorman, "of happy memory," as we said, unloosed on me during the Candidacy: "I can't stand Chuck. I just can't *stand* him." That was exceedingly bad form, even between friends, as both Gorman and I immediately recognized, and it is more than certain that Brother Gorman's next examination of conscience fed voraciously on that extraordinary judgment on one of his fellow Novices.

What charity had more difficulty with was the climate between Brother Gorman and myself that encouraged that heartfelt exclamation. It did not take me or anyone else very long in that greenhouse to decide who was quick and who was dead; who was bright and who dim; who was a fan and who preferred paddleball. In the World we would have sorted ourselves out accordingly, and called it friendship. But if charity deftly undermined enmity, it was not particularly keen on friendship, except in that deep spiritual sense that meant nothing. To no avail. No force on earth or in heaven could prevent me from privately liking Brother Scally or Brother Brennan or Brother Flynn and publicly preferring their company. The Novitiate ideal of charity, of loving all equally, seemed willing to yield on the internal question and concentrated instead on the public manifestations of equal-handed treatment. Thus the constant emphasis on "mixing" and the sometimes painful institution of as-signed bands.

Some of us were in fact friends and we silently acknowledged it by unobtrusively but delightedly seeking out each other's company when the circumstances were socially fluid enough to permit it. Some possibly had no social preferences at all or else were so sanctified that they allowed the randomness of intercourse to prevail everywhere and at all times. If that was so, it was truly heroic virtue and, as it seems even now, almost inhuman. Surely Brother Suchard and Brother Zweifel preferred the company of Brother Geller, who would speak to them of the Sacred Heart, to mine, where they would have to listen to remarks about their native city, whatever that should chance to be, and at which a perfect charity would constrain them to smile. Or was Brother Geller, *terribile dictu,* a bore for all seasons? Only Brother Suchard knew and the odds are prohibitively high that he will carry the secret to his frozen grave in North Tonawanda.

Without the social softener of charity, the taut fabric of the Novitiate would have been rent in a week. It is easier to see that now than it was then, but that is not what concerned us then either. We were far more interested in a related but slightly different phenomenon that the spiritual readings called "Particular Friendships." At first a "particular friend," a PF in the Novitiate vernacular, seemed to be someone like Jack Scally or even Tom Connolly who was, God help me, *solid* but with whom I could swap news, gossip and speculation with some expectation of a sympathetic response. But only at first. A "particular friend" was indeed "particular," as it turned out.

I knew quite literally nothing about homosexuality at

age eighteen. In high school there were frequent jokes about "fruits." What we were laughing at was effeminate behavior, but I doubt if any of us who told of or laughed about limp wrists, peculiar gaits and lisping speech ever connected any of it with either general or specific sexual behavior with another male. The Jesuits themselves seemed unconcerned. In their high schools of that era boys played all the female roles, at times in strikingly realistic fashion, in school plays, and sometimes from their freshman to their senior year. Some of those players were effeminate and some were probably homosexuals, though unlikely then of a practicing sort. And some of them were accepted into the Society of Jesus: I journeyed to St. Andrew with a perfectly lovely Portia.

It is even less likely that anyone approaching St. Andrew had had a deliberate homosexual experience than that he had had a heterosexual one. And the endless struggle against concupiscence, which began as a skirmish in grammar school, had broken out into open warfare in high school and was still going on as a kind of "cold war" in the Novitiate, was invariably against the heterosexual variety. If there were homosexuals in the Novitiate, their concupiscence was not hidden in a closet but buried in a storm cellar, and likely buried so deeply that neither they nor anyone else could detect it.

We were all supposed to be sexually disengaged in the Jesuits, and, masturbation apart, whose frequency I have no way of even guessing, I suppose that pretty nearly everyone was. The prospect of confessing even sexual misdemeanors (a category almost nonexistent in canon law, which took a decidedly felonious view of all sexual

behavior) was not an appetizing one. Some of the Novices
were probably sexually disinterested, or pretty near so, as
well as disengaged: they had no visible curiosity about
women, looked as if they never had and never would.

I say this now with no greater conviction than I had
then. Sex was an absolutely forbidden topic of conversation, and who knows what thoughts were coursing
through those apparently disinterested heads? But if any
did yield to sexual fantasies, it is unlikely that they were
homosexual ones, such was the severe taboo that gripped
that subject in the Catholic world of that time.

No, the problem was a different one: heterosexuals
grappling with subtle sexual urges that could, effortlessly
and almost unobserved, come to rest on another male.
What was latent at St. Andrew was sexuality pure and
simple, and the "particular friendships" of the spiritual
reading were nothing more or less than male relationships
tinged with eroticism. No one spoke that word; no one
even suggested it. But to observe the relationship was to
understand it, and to experience it was to understand it
absolutely. No, it was not Brother Scally and Brother
Flynn that the good Rodríguez had in mind but the likes
of Brothers Driscoll or O'Mara, those cute little boys who
were every whit as boring as Christopher Looney, the
lunatic liturgist, but in whose peculiarly attractive company one somehow found oneself with increasing frequency.

It was an eerie, exciting and disturbing experience,
those coy courtships of ephebes with blue eyes and golden
curls. You knew what was happening and yet you did
not. You knew the relationship had a peculiar quality
about it, a kind of urgency that other friendships did not

possess. And yet we had at our disposal neither the linguistic nor the conceptual framework exactly to identify it, except that when a PF was being discussed, we all knew precisely what was meant. There were friends and "friends," and the latter were clearly erotic adventures, though only rarely recognized precisely as such by the young men caught up in them.

Brothers Driscoll and O'Mara were mere catnip, pretty boys upon whom nature had bestowed a physical grace that appeared feminine in that all-male society. They were probably all garden-variety heterosexuals whose naiveté and innocence generally prevented them from picking up the vaguely erotic signals being beamed in their direction. But occasionally there was a response, a faint blip on one party's or the other's sexual radar. We all thought we had pulled the plug on that delicate instrument when we entered the Novitiate, but the Master, Padre Rodríguez and even the Desert Fathers in their opaque Coptic way understood that the controls might be moved from Overt to Subliminal but that they could never be turned to Off. A Particular Friendship was in the making.

At first those relationships were easy, if noticeable, but they later grew urgent, then exclusive, then careful and finally furtive. In that world of deliberate threes—*numquam duo* shone out like a blazon on our foreheads—an actual duo stood out like a Presbyterian. The principals were forced underground; that is, they ostentatiously avoided each other at the common recreation but conspired to meet alone and unobserved at other times. But no one could so contrive in that glassy compound, and so they became all the more remarkable.

When erotic attachments did develop, they were only

remotely physical. The Rule of Touch, that enigma that had been unveiled to us in the Candidacy, now explicitly interposed itself to curb ardor before it became overtly sexual. "Don't touch!" shouted Rodríguez, *"Noli tangere!,"* with an inspired understanding of Jesus' words to Mary Magdalen at the tomb in John 20:17. Now at last both Rule and Gospel became clear: Don't touch Brother Driscoll!

The Rule of Touch was not the cure, however. The true cure was peer pressure, social conformity and the growing awareness in the "friends'" own consciences that what they were so single-mindedly about was not only awkward but possibly dangerous as well. The social life of the Novitiate was not very elastic to begin with, and to circumvent its narrowly prescribed limits extraordinary measures had to be taken, like resorting to odd places at odd times. Being observed under such circumstances was almost inevitable, and so there was always the possibility that someone like Brother Houghton, who innocently thought that only charity was being violated by their behavior, might blurt out something explosively innocuous at a Particular Chapter or into the Master's private ear. "Manifestation" hung like an ominous and fatal sword over the heads of "particular friends."

The attachments never survived for very long. Though the Novitiate taboo against the direct and the personal forbade the possibility of saying anything to the principals, there was an uneasy and almost embarrassed disapproval of their conduct, not on moral grounds, surely, since no one even dared think of that aspect of the relationship, but because in their presence we had all become intruders. These odd pairs, by becoming exclusive to each other, denied themselves to the rest of us. It was uncomfortable and so it was unacceptable.

The blossoming of the Particular Friendship in this revealing erotic mode was a Novitiate phenomenon; in the Juniorate, where social intercourse was much freer and the opportunity for privacy greater, such exotic growths were almost unknown and never recurred thereafter. Relationships became more relaxed and more natural as the course progressed. Oddly, once given a free choice, we actually preferred to "mix." Charity turned out to be a far more natural instinct than any of us imagined when as Novices we were struggling so desperately to acquire it.

IV

Observance

We were a most peculiar company. We lived in spec-
tacularly close quarters under the unremitting glare of the
Master and each other, yet in the deepest personal
isolation. For me at least, the isolation did not breed
loneliness nor a longing for the life I had so casually left
behind me. Those prescribed and detailed Novitiate tasks
that flowed endlessly out of the Regular Order filled my
days and spread into my thoughts and fantasies. At
meditation I might lapse into a reverie about that day's
work assignments or tomorrow's softball game but never
about how wonderful it would be to return to the Bronx.
If I missed anything, it was the ability to communicate
immediately those awesomely devastating insights I rou-
tinely harvested in the course of scrubbing the showers or
polishing the woodwork. Many of us fancied ourselves as
Oscar Wildes, I'm sure, and, like poor Oscar at Reading

Gaol, we had to save our deathless quips for recreation with the inmates after lunch and dinner.

But recreation, like all else, unfolded in a social climate not of our own making. Most societies sort themselves into some kind of ranked hierarchy, a pecking order based on a perceptible difference in behavior, abilities, function, appearance or inherited status. This natural segregation into groups, clans, households or cliques was expressly forbidden us by the religious ideal of charity. We were to be, in another of the Master's favorite phrases, shamelessly cribbed from Saint Paul, "all things to all men," which, in the Novitiate's perverse exegetical tradition, meant that we were to treat each of our peers in an exactly identical fashion.

In a real sense the Novitiate was a classless society within a larger Society of Jesus riddled with distinctions of both class and caste. Juniors were a class apart from Novices, and the Lay Brothers were located an unbridgeable caste distance away from all of us. As Novices we all wore the same clothes, shared the same tasks and suffered identical privations. The Master might confer some status on the Manuductor and other minor functionaries, but it was so transparently delegated and so ephemeral that it was effectively no status at all.

There were special tasks, to be sure: some Novices were chosen to play Angels over a summer or lead a procession or take charge of cutting down a tree. A great deal of energy was expended on discerning the rationale behind such choices, but the Master was far ahead of us. As soon as we thought we could see a pattern in those microscopic dispensations, the Master's cunning finger would move on and inexplicably confer a small pat on the head of the likes of Brother Hickman, who was much admired for his insouciant bravado with the dishwashing machine but whom few of his peers would have entrusted with the correct time. In that most predictable of all worlds, nothing was predictable.

So if the Master and the Regular Order resolutely refused to confer status in some recognizable way, we did it ourselves. There were, beyond the jerks and jitters of gait and costume, real differences of behavior and abilities among the Novice population, and each lined them up in whatever order he had arranged his own priorities. Whatever the Master might or might not do or say, nothing could dissuade me that Mr. Battistessa was Very Superior Stuff, that Brother Whelan was already as smart and Brother Zimmer as dumb as any of us was ever likely to become or that Brother Dromgool had toppled down from another planet. The difficulty was, there was neither an official nor even a consensual recognition of the various status orders that emerged. They existed only in the head of each of us and were only occasionally and cautiously shared.

The problem lay not in identifying and saluting the swift and the brave and the bright, but in the value-laden domain of observance. Some of the Novices were, to the eye and the ear at least, more observant of the letter and the spirit of what was being presented to us as the Jesuit or, better, the Novitiate ideal of behavior. But if these were the true aristocrats of the system, there were no real rewards for them, neither external perquisites nor the visible and universal esteem of their fellows. The system itself refused to confer the external rewards, and we had no way of publicly registering whatever esteem we may have felt.

My own feelings were very mixed. On my private scale of values, some of the Grand Masters of Observance were mere dim-witted obscurantists, while others were genuinely admirable heroes of a difficult spiritual combat. But I shared none of that esteem or lack of it with its subjects; as Grand Masters they would not have tolerated such wildly unobservant judgments on my part. What followed was almost inevitable: my value judgments could be shared only with Less Than Grand Observants, a communications channel whose limitations tended to debase observance.

Some sense had to be made of all of this. Each measured his own perceptions, and the like-dispositioned made dialectical attempts at rendering it intelligible at recreation. It was the Master of Novices, however, who gave the official interpretation of what the Jesuit life was all about. He did it first by assuming the impossible task of being the perfect Novice, a burden that would have crushed most Jesuit Fathers in the course of a single long afternoon. To be the focus of seventy-five pairs of youthfully acute eyes bent on ferreting out the slightest suggestion that *you* were not what you were asking *them* to be meant that you really had to be the Perfect Novice, root and branch, essence and existence. And Robert Grissom, S.J., to his credit, was. He was our role model, and if it was a lousy role, he was a flawless model. He was a stern, almost humorless, self-demanding and single-minded man, and he turned out, at least for the nonce, a number of pretty fair simulacra.

He expressed how the Life worked in our morning conferences, where he glossed the Rules and traditions of the Society of Jesus. His presentation was, like all else he did, low-key, controlled and unembellished by either fervor or rhetoric. There were remarkably few allusions in those conferences, no edges where the Master's own experiences or reading shone out from under his direct but abstract presentation of the virtues of the Jesuit life. All the "preceding" could indeed have been "confirmed by example," and of the most contemporary kind, but he chose not to titillate us in this manner. It would clearly have smacked of "personalities" to have discussed even the most anonymous Jesuit behavior that fell short of perfect observance. We were left to supply our own examples of virtuous shortfalls, drawn necessarily, and perhaps designedly, from our own lives.

The Master's favorite virtue was simplicity, which he probably possessed, but which left most of his patient and extremely attentive audience perplexed. Many of the Novices notable for their careful observance of the Rules appeared to me to be simple-minded rather than simple, and if that was what the Master of Novices had in mind for the rest of us, the prospect was both frightening and, at base, implausible.

Equally implausible were the classic Jesuit role models of the seventeenth century, Saint John Berchmans, N.S.J., an apple-cheeked Belgian boy who died in the Novitiate, possibly before he reached puberty, and Saint

Aloysius Gonzaga, S.J., an Italian of illustrious family who made it a little further into the course before toppling over from quartan ague or some such other seventeenth-century disease. Berchmans seemed like a rather prissy cartoon and had his unattractive contemporary counterparts, while Gonzaga, whose chastity (or lack of it) was such that he spurned even to look upon his mother after he had taken vows, was such an exotic bloom that he was simply set aside as sui generis.

What the grotesque Gonzaga was about, when he was not busy curbing his murderous Italian temper, was a popular Jesuit exercise known as "custody of the senses," keeping the voice and the body and the curiosity under tight control. The various subspecies of "custody of the senses" were popular areas of self-improvement, probably because they were virtues of tone and style rather than substance and so could be used freely in all the areas of self-accusation in which we were necessarily engaged. The most popular of all, because it was the most difficult and at the same time transparently innocuous, was "modesty of the eyes," which meant that we did not stare wildly about from either impertinence or unwonted (a popular Jesuit word) curiosity. Instead, the eyes were to be kept demurely cast down on some imaginary spot on the ground about three feet in front of you.

The intent of "custody of the senses" was not so much to make us appear unassuming as to instill control and composure. We glided around the halls like leashed samurai, head straight ahead at all times, the eyes cast down, the gait regular and calm. The bearing was not military but *modest,* precisely. There was to be no broad gesticulation, no slumping or slouching, no undue (or unwonted) raising of the voice. Converting adolescents into Stoics in the full grip of *apatheia* was not an easy task, but the social pressure and example were enormously effective, and within a month even the most brutish Novice had stopped contorting and howling, all save Brother Dromgool, who *always* stared about with wild abandon. It may have been his thin sight or, more likely, a constant and total amazement at what was going on around him.

We may have become behavioral Stoics, but we did not spend much time philosophizing. The Master deplored idle speculation, as he called it, and his anti-intellectual attitudes crept through every sentence of his bland conferences. Though none of us was quite sure exactly what was involved, we did know that after these two years of the First Probation we would be launched upon a twelve-year course of studies and that most of us would end up as some kind of teacher. The Master seemed almost regretful at the prospect. He knew perhaps, and as we would discover, that the "simple" of the Novitiate would be also-rans in a race that would begin as soon as we walked out of his conference room and the Novitiate, and that his beloved "simplicity" was not an exceedingly negotiable currency in the Jesuit faculty rooms of Fordham or Loyola or Holy Cross.

Was Robert Grissom, S.J., an also-ran? He was teaching and living one Jesuit ideal, an authentic one perhaps, though it was sometimes difficult to connect it with the intent of the founding Fathers, while our own limited experience, the history of the Order and the privileged atmosphere of the other, Juniorate side of this same house was silently preaching quite another—that of the scholar-intellectual, the subtle and learned Jesuit who knocked them dead at the Council of Trent and who still supplied whatever theological acumen managed to penetrate the Roman Curia, the Society of Jesus of Jean Daniélou, Teilhard de Chardin and Karl Rahner.

Discharged from the Master's conference, we struggled for self-knowledge, and there were some nicely calibrated Jesuit instruments to thrust it upon us. We examined our conscience twice daily, before lunch and late in the evening, when we stood at the side of our desks, collected ourselves, bent down and kissed the floor, and then for the space of fifteen minutes reviewed our actions since the last examen. To assist in the bookkeeping, each had at hand a tiny notebook in which he entered the number, though never the names, of his faults since the last examen, and in this way instructive comparisons could be drawn at the end of the day, the week, the month. For those who savored the *delictum in flagrante,* there was even a little string of beads—"*culpa* beads"—which could be pinned vertically to the inside breast pocket of the soutane. When you apprehended yourself in your favorite vice—"I'm working on charity this week"—you simply reached inside the cassock and moved a bead from the top to the bottom of your moral abacus. No wonder we were exhausted at night.

We all went to confession, though not very often, and to the Master himself. This did not seem to me like a very apt forum (nor even a very canonical one, it was later whispered) for a discussion of human passions or my consuming and continuous dislike for Brother Suchard, who was observant and so could not conceivably be unlikable, or my intolerance of Brother Gilligan, who was not very observant and so might be done some grievous harm by my calling unnecessary attention to him. No, not with the Master. I had to straighten myself out and pray against all hope that someone else would straighten out Brothers Suchard and Gilligan, whose vile habits were obviously at the root of the problem.

That someone else might be their "admonitor." Admonition grew out of the strenuously preached and deeply felt responsibility we owed to one another in charity. We were our brothers' keepers, but to prevent this Christian and fraternal duty from lapsing directly into mayhem it was parceled out in a carefully controlled way. Gossip or a private discussion of someone else's faults was held to be in very bad form, but you could tell the principal to his face, if you were his official admonitor. Each of us had a randomly assigned admonitor, who was changed every couple of months either to give each of us a different perspective or, more likely, to avoid the possibility of a bloodbath.

There was an admonition period once a week for about fifteen minutes. It was signaled, as was everything else, by the sound of a bell. You stood patiently and modestly at your desk in the ascetory until your admonitor approached. He told you, in English for a more perfect understanding, the inappropriate things he had noted in your behavior during the past week. You thanked him and then went off to discharge the same charitable duty on your assigned victim.

It was not a particularly revealing exercise, perhaps because it was so personal and direct. You could not stand there and tell Brother Gilligan to his face that he should wash more often; it was simply too painful. Nor could you inform Brother Suchard that he was, not to put too fine a point on it, obnoxious; the charge was too cosmic, too metaphysical, for all its transparent truth. So we called each other's attention to motes, quirks and fidgets, the small print in the Rules. The premise, which no one bought, of course, was that everything else was terrific, Gonzagalike, one might say.

There were moments, however. Brother Sims was another of those unspoiled young men from the frozen north—what kind of crazy high school were Ours running in Buffalo anyway, I often thought. The genus Snow Owl seemed to come in two varieties, smiling-smiling (*species* Brother Zweifel) and smiling-dour (*species* Brother Suchard), though each was plumb-straight and rotten at heart. Brother Sims was smiling-smiling, and if he disapproved of the antics of his big-city brothers, he kept his feelings on the subject well under invisible control. We took turns trying to boggle the innocent Brother Sims— had he heard that the Master was married and fathered twins before he became a Jesuit?—but he never turned a hair on his neatly trimmed head, secure, perhaps, in the knowledge that he was a paradigm of observance.

One evening I had to perform one of the little exercises calculated gently to remind the Novices that we would not be scrubbing latrines and dry-mopping corridors for the rest of our lives. There was a novena to the Sacred Heart in progress, and on each of the nine evenings one of the Novices delivered a modest sermon to his wondering peers in the chapel. My topic was "Heart of Jesus, in whom are all the treasures of wisdom and knowledge" (a very near-miss from the opaque "Heart of Jesus, desire of the everlasting hills," whatever *that* meant), and I did my fifteen minutes in a manner so elegant, so learned yet moving, so pious yet sober as to suggest that Fulton Sheen had best pack his eye-liner and seek out a new career preaching to deaf mutes in Calcutta.

At the next day's admonition Brother Sims approached my desk without his usual sunny smile. My God, was he about to unload Something Big? Had he seen dimly through the lines of that sermon that *I* was *his* future in a world where sunny smiles and perfect observance loomed not half so large, and so had come to dispatch me before the menace grew too large? No, it was sadder and truer than that. "Brother," he began, uncertain where to start on such an enormous subject, "why is it that you can talk like that but that you're not that way at all?"

It sounded like a question, but I had been admonished, modestly, almost offhandedly, but in precisely that cosmic way I never thought possible or likely. Admonition was not supposed to be a debate; you were to listen and not retort or defend. I did neither. I thanked Brother Sims, who smiled his sunny smile once again and went happily off to hear a rehearsal of his own inconsequential faults. I stood there a very long time, shaken at last by Ronald Sims, N.S.J. No, I was *not* that way at all.

Admonition fell under the rubric of fraternal correction, an obligation we owed each other in Christ, but one which had obviously to be administered with great discretion if any of us was to survive. When it became particularly delicate was when it was delivered not at deskside but in public fora. The General Chapter was probably nothing more than myth, a communal truth-telling session wherein each voiced his general observations about Novitiate discipline in the presence of the Master. It was described in the Rules, but no one had ever experienced or even heard of one meeting. The Particular Chapter was all too real, however. It occurred about once a month, unannounced, when we convened for our daily conference. The Master cleared his throat, smiled and summoned one of the Novices to kneel, hands clasped and head penitently bent, in the middle of the conference room. Then, with a nod from the Master, each Novice in turn stood and noted what was worthy of correction in the subject's observance.

The danger was probably less real than it first seemed. Everyone had an innate glimmer of the limits of this exercise, and even the insanely pious would be unlikely publicly to accuse someone of masturbation, of sleeping during meditation, of talking after lights out or of other heinous and capital crimes. They might wound, but they would never kill. How one's friends would react was more interesting. It was perfectly acceptable to say "Haven't noticed anything, Father" when one's turn came, and to offer that in the instance of someone truly despicable was much admired by the cognoscenti, since the Master doubtless knew he was being had. But to say it of a known and notorious friend was bad form and greeted with derision in later, more private moments. The admirable thing to do in the case of one's friends was to cite a vice that was really a virtue. "Brother is somewhat overzealous in his charity, Father" was bold, perhaps overly so, and even the Master had his limits. Being overscrupulous about anything was good, and, failing all imagination, violation of modesty of the eyes was always an acceptable if impoverished accusation in a Particular Chapter.

Dangers arose from unexpected quarters on occasion. Brother Monahan was a naive and amusing child, even in a society of eighteen-year-olds. When he arose in his turn at one Particular Chapter, it was expected that he might say something naive or amusing, if he wasn't paralyzed with fear.

"Brother O'Leary doesn't observe the Rules, Father."

The silence was absolute. The Master's vein popped a good inch out of his forehead. He smiled very, very slowly, the light glinting off his rimless glasses. We were approaching the End of the World. The kneeling Brother O'Leary was alleged not to have a vocation.

"What do you mean, Brother Monahan?"

In an instant Brother Monahan ended his brief career as a naif. Some enormous new understanding had come upon him.

"I don't know, Father. . . . Nothing."

Two days later Brother Monahan was no longer with us. Possibly he was in his native Jersey City, but it would not have defied belief if he lay buried in the midst of a cornfield in Iowa.

Where fraternal correction was more terrifying was where it arose not from ritual but passed from one Novice to the Master to you. God only knew what the Manuductor reported to the Master or what spilled forth from conscience or guilt-addled tongues in that spartan tank across the hall. "Manifestation," the disclosure to the Superior of the faults of others, was urged by the Rule, but the youthful American soul cried out that it was patently finking, ratting on a colleague. And yet *manifestatio* was a duly indited part of the system, its most notorious and unappetizing element, perhaps, and so there was no protest in principle. Just hope.

When the bad news came, it came with the suddenness of an earthquake.

"*Pater Magister vult te videre.*" The Master wants to see you.

"*Me?*"

"*Te.*"

This particular summons, which might be delivered by the Manuductor or by the last visitor to the Master's office, was popularly known as a vult, and all the gallows humor about the ult vult and high vultage did not lessen the horror of its arrival. No one ever thought it heralded good news. Rather, the mind raced over the familiar terrain of transgression and guilt. What would this one be for? The effect was frequently cathartic. Not even the Master could replicate my own catalogue of bad moves, and so it was unlikely that he could deliver the kind of blow I had already dealt myself on my way out of the ascetory into the hall.

The vult look was transparent and well known. Friends could observe the delivery of the brief message as I sat at my desk staring eyeless at my Kempis and could follow my thoughtful and funereal progress across the ascetory.

A pair of fingers was slowly raised to form a V. A nod. A returned nod of encouragement.

"Come in." The Master always spoke the vernacular.

The Master stood there in his white T-shirt and black trousers. His cassock lay on the bed. My God, this was going to be bad: he had interrupted himself. The heavy odor of cigar smoke hung in the room.

"Sit down, Brother."

A quick glance at the desk. Nothing there, no scroll, edict or writ of execution. Eyes quickly averted directly ahead. There was the confessional prie-dieu, the purple stole draped over it—shall I confess all immediately?—and, above, the preposterous tiny red spot just at eye level when you knelt. Legend said it was blood but differed as to whether it was the Master's, splattered forth from his tattered back during a frenzy of flagellation, or a consumptive Novice's, coughed up during the throes of a final but all-healing confession.

"You seem to have visitors downstairs, Brother."

The breath seeps out between clenched teeth. The pulse drops, spirits rise.

"This is not a visiting day, Brother."

"Yes, I know. I have no idea who they are, Father."

I can handle this. Unsummoned visitors from New York City have the same moral declension as nocturnal emissions. I wonder who it is.

"Well, you'd better go down and see them. But please inform them of the visiting regulations."

"Yes, of course, Father."

Out of there and into a visitor's cassock, which is almost clean and almost fits. Anxiety is dropping off me like tropical sweat. First touch base with Brother Scally, who had flashed the reassuring nod in the ascetory.

"*Adsunt hospites.*" Visitors.

"*Hospites?* Is that all?"

"Yeah."

Relief doth make English speakers of us all.

V

Meditation and Other Trials

One item of the Regular Order never varied: from 6 to 7 A.M. we meditated. On the previous evening, shortly before retiring, we prepared our "points" for the next morning's meditation. The Angels had done this for us during the Candidacy and the Master every day during the Long Retreat and occasionally thereafter. It was not very complicated. You selected an appropriate text, something from the next day's Mass, perhaps, and developed it. You imagined the setting, if it was a Gospel scene, for instance, and went over what happened and what was said. You tried to extract some personal lesson from it, some issue that would improve your observance or further your spiritual development. The Master was strong on generosity—"God loves a generous giver"— and so I suppose there was a great deal of generosity of spirit being meditated on those dark mornings.

Rising at five-thirty was never easy, no matter what time I went to bed. It was a physically tiring life with its intense concentration and continual but often interrupted work. Now it is appalling to think of stumbling upstairs, in line, of course, from the chapel to the dark and frigid ascetory with breakfast and coffee still two hours away. Then, somehow, my still-young nervous system adjusted to the coffee privation but found it hard to stay awake for an hour, even on pained knees. Nor was I the only one who found it difficult, as I could observe in the deep morning gloom of the ascetory. Heads nodded, backs arched and bent, weight was shifted from one knee to the other. You could rise and stand for a space, if that helped, though it was not highly regarded. No one ever *said* anything: the silent example of the bellwethers of observance, who *never* stood, was enough. You could even sit during meditation, if you had the nerve. The fictive presumption was that you had spinal cancer, but it had better clear up the next day.

Meditation was difficult. I was told that once I developed calluses on my knees, as sure enough I did, it would be easier. It wasn't. It was still difficult to kneel, to stay awake, to keep the mind focused. I daydreamed, mused, fantasized, counted the days to the next holiday, to the end of the Novitiate. I watched Brother Houghton in front of me, knees riveted in place on the kneeler, back absolutely straight, head and shoulders motionless. I checked out Brother O'Leary near the wall. Aha, sitting! Scally was doing well; no great motion there. Maguire was nodding. That was OK: he was *solid*. Brother Leahy in the gloom of the far corner was kneeling perfectly erect. Houghtonesque, his head bent and turned slightly to the side. He was not nodding; he was *meditating*.

Brother Leahy escaped the Novitiate in the most cunning way imaginable: he was high for nearly two years. Some of us could manage it for a few days or even for a week every six months or so, but clever old Matt went up on the Long Retreat and didn't descend until he took his vows nearly two years later. It was an astonishing display of what all the masters of the spiritual life called "consolation," a euphoric state which comes suddenly and transforms the basest Novice into a golden paradigm of observance and piety. In the full grip of consolation one can kneel and meditate for hours. Charity comes out of the pores. Appetite abates. Sweet converse becomes easy, even with the likes of Brothers Looney and Suchard.

The spiritual guidebooks knew all about consolation. It was said to do no great harm—something that pleasant must do *some* harm—though the Evil Spirit sometimes sends it to tempt us to excess (fat chance!). But we were warned not to expect it to last, not unless you were Brother Leahy. He arrived at St. Andrew a mischievous Irish kid, not exceedingly bright (he went to St. Peter's Prep, the Jersey alma mater of the late lamented Brother Monahan and the Dade County Community College of the Jesuit academic pecking order), but he was energetic, entertaining and had a nice innocence upon him. Consolation attacked Brother Leahy, overwhelmed him, during that first long October. His head tilted ominously and his face suddenly saddened into the mien of piety. There were no more jokes, just wan smiles. He developed a nicely ascetic cough, somewhere between spiritual nervousness and consumption. Sighs exploded from him. His conversation was impeccable; his industry and scrupulosity in work were a marvel to attend. He became, in short, unbearable.

Except that most of us could remember him before his marvelous transformation and so could not take the new Brother Leahy entirely seriously. A Suchard or a Brother Geller arrived at the Novitiate already swathed in piety; Matt Leahy's mistake, or his salvation, was that he put his on in full view of his friends, who were rather more amused than impressed. Everyone knew Matt would land. We just did not understand how he stayed up so long.

We all envied Brother Leahy. He may have become a pain in the ass to his fellows, but we all knew how easy some things had become for him, particularly meditation. Even I knew that floating sensation when you cannot even feel your knees beneath you on the unyielding kneeler and when your mind dwells on Jesus Feeding the Multitudes (God is a generous giver, why not me?) as if it were welded there. It was pure transport, and it was that which separated Brother Houghton in front of me from Brother Leahy across the ascetory. Brother Houghton was merely observant in that dim and unastonishing way that froze the spirit. There was no transport about him. Brother Leahy reeked transport, and, possibly and deliciously, consumption.

Solid Brother Maguire was now in full drowse, as he would be every morning for the four years he was exposed to my immodest gaze. Sleepy but *solid*. Brother

F. X. O'Brien (like Johnsons in the National Basketball Association, the multitude of Jesuit O'Briens had to be sorted out by initial) was standing under the brightly illuminated ascetory clock that ticked off, in full view of all, every terrible minute of that terrible hour. He was not only standing; he was fidgeting and looking out the ascetory window at the gradually lightening landscape outside. F. X. O'Brien was fat and flabby, and kneeling must have been a horror for him. Sports certainly were, because he hated them, and meals were, too, because he loved them. The ideal Novice was a mediocre but serviceable athlete with little appetite and a penchant for woodcutting. F. X. O'Brien had none of those Master virtues; he had only appetites and no yet discernible skills. More, it was Lent and he was probably thinking about lunch instead of Jesus Feeding the Multitudes.

At lunchtime, now a mere light-year away, we would all file into the refectory and deprive ourselves of the one tolerated creature comfort in the Novitiate, eating. Jesuit life was hardly ascetic by anyone's standards, save possibly a Dominican's. It discouraged the rough and tough stuff, and though it was intimated that later on we would be on our own and so could indulge whatever privations of the flesh we chose, whip and chain whenever we chose, the message came down that hairshirt and hacksaw were not the Jesuit style, and certainly not in the Novitiate. Nobody was pushing indulgence, assuredly; moderation was the keynote, with advice to take in or let go a little in season.

For a Novice there was not much room to let go, except with food. We all ate well and we all gained weight and muscle in the new regime of fresh air, exercise and wholesome food. Lent was the season for taking in, again at table. If meat was proscribed on certain days by Canon Law, the cook took care of that. But fasting was up to each individual. It was generally expected that during Lent you fasted at lunch—it was forbidden at dinner—and the callow bolted lunch in about five minutes with a glow of self-satisfaction upon them and trailing the disdain of the aficionados of virtue. The pious professional ate less, but he dawdled over it so as not to seem to be fasting overly severely. F. X. O'Brien usually bolted, though without disdain. Everyone understood that the sight of uneaten food was simply too much for him to bear. Already at six-thirty in the morning he was probably shedding a fat tear for the lovely tuna salad he would not eat six hours later.

F. X. O'Brien spoke openly and engagingly about his appetites. It was an indulgence he permitted himself and others permitted to him because it seemed so innocent. He could prattle on about food, and Brother Gilligan could expose his mania for sports, but most of the Novices kept their appetites and manias well concealed. Moderation translated very nicely into cool, and if F. X. O'Brien and Brother Gilligan had no cool, the rest of us had enough to reach to Buffalo and back. The Regular Order and walking in file probably promoted the long view of things, and the sheer physical closeness made some kind of distancing inevitable. We all lived together a very long time and knew nothing about one another. In all our talk the purely personal rarely surfaced. What each's doubts, fears and anxieties were, only each knew. What we really thought about this life, this vocation, no one revealed, even to his closest friends.

The personal was only one realm of the unspoken. We never talked about women or sex, of course. There was no obscenity, even of the perfunctory kind, and no scatology. It took four years of Jesuit life for "crap" to rise to someone's lips and another three for "shit." "Fucking," even in its modest adjectival form, never made it. We joked about the Jesuits incessantly, but never about the Church. We joked about each other and of course about the Master of Novices, though the latter subject never raised much of a smile in certain quarters. Some were presumably reserving their laughter for the first breaking out of the Beatific Vision.

We were innocents living in a pre-therapeutic age, unaccustomed to self-revelation in any form. It occurred to no one of us that he should be "in touch with his feelings" and much less that he should spread them around for others' inspection. It was not repression; it was a matter of habit and form. For me, personal matters were almost always moral matters. There was simply no separating the two. I had not discussed morality with my parents, and I was not about to begin now with these others. The confessional had trained me to empty my moral bowels on command and in place.

Here in the Novitiate the moral valorization of daily experience ran even deeper. Everything, every act, every thought, could be viewed through the prism of the Rules and thence inevitably connected with the ultimate question: Do I have a vocation? Am I called to this life? We were all there on the presumption that we had and we were. To weigh those questions a thousand times daily was impossible, and so we devalorized some small part of our experience, which we could then safely talk about, and left the rest unsaid. That was what Brother Monahan did not understand.

Nor would he ever explain. Brother Monahan and Brothers Gorman and Toland, my earlier companions on the New York Central, and a number of others all disappeared from St. Andrew and our lives in an almost identical fashion: one morning they were simply not there. None had taken vows and so needed no official release; they vacated quickly and quietly, like ghosts. The swiftness and silence of separation was probably official policy on the Master's part. There were no public explanations, of course, and no time for private revelations, and so to this day I have no idea of who asked to leave and who was dismissed from the Novitiate, on what grounds or after what kind of discussions.

At first the departure of acquaintances was merely a curiosity, the subject of some brief and cautious comments at recreation, no more. But as our common bonds grew thicker with shared experiences, it was no longer acquaintances but friends who left us. They left spaces behind them. Yet even these filled up remarkably quickly. Our life was so self-contained and discontinuous with the World outside that these former friends almost ceased to exist, not in the grievous manner of the dead, but in the oblivious manner of someone who had suddenly moved to California.

At six-forty-five I felt as if I were slowly being crushed into the kneeler beneath me. Enough. I had made it this far. I stood up. Below, in the covered walkway leading to the chapel, I could see Mr. Battistessa, S.J., strolling majestically up and down. Juniors were permitted unspeakable privileges, like going out and meditating on the porticos and walkway. The walkway was called the Via Regis, and Battistessa was indeed regal, an Italian peacock in black; dark curls glistening under his biretta; white French cuffs shot perfectly forth from under his immaculate cassock. No one knew how he managed to look the dandy in issued clerical clothes, but manage it he did, and now he proceeded languidly toward the chapel with the assurance of the Rector himself and all the radiant elegance of a newly minted monsignor from Queens.

The Manuductor rang a small bell on his desk ten minutes before the hour, and we all rose and headed down to the chapel for Mass. The single file of Juniors and Novices descending from their separate wings of the house met at its center and marched in silence and with downcast eyes along the left and right sides of the Via Regis into the chapel, Juniors left, Novices right, one pew filling after the next. The chapel bell sounded seven o'clock, and the Fathers in the community filed left and right out of the sacristy with their servers to say their own private Masses in the alcoves along the aisles of the chapel. Last of all issued the Rector to celebrate Mass at the main altar for the assembled Novices and Juniors.

The Reverend George Flattery, S.J., looked like a Rector, or possibly a diplomat or a college president, a tall and erect man with gray hair and a face gracefully contoured by the suggestion of good living. I think I had very mixed feelings about our Rector, a man with whom

I had never exchanged a word—or was ever likely to—but whose graceful, well-tailored and well-coifed figure I observed every single morning for eighteen months. Secretly I fancied a Rector who looked like Ronald Colman, just as I fancied and envied Mr. Battistessa's dark Italian elegance. But I had also unwittingly absorbed some of the Master's disdain for sleek worldliness, and I and others shared an unvoiced judgment that the Rector was very likely a lightweight. Perhaps he was, but my theorem on his worldliness was suddenly left in ruin when it was announced that the Reverend George Flattery, S.J., was departing for the missions.

Every Jesuit province had an assigned overseas missionary territory to which it supplied personnel and funds. It had been so from the beginning when early Jesuits went out and dazzled the wits out of Chinese emperors, Japanese shoguns and Akbar the Great Mogul. The longtime mission of the New York Province was the Philippine Islands, probably a legacy of the Spanish-American War when the Spanish Jesuits there were expelled and replaced by their American counterparts. The Philippines were a very Catholic and civilized place and so it was hardly a hardship post for a New York Jesuit, just a long way from home. But immediately after World War II the New York Province received another political legacy from the Pope, the Pacific Islands Trust Territory. It wasn't Darkest Africa, but it would obviously do for those who thirsted for the missionary field.

In theory anyone could be sent to the missions, but in practice one volunteered. It was piously believed (a code expression for a Novice consensus) that there were many more volunteers for the missions than there were places in those thatched huts, but no one knew for sure, a piece of ignorance that seriously inhibited impetuous gestures. Novices lived on impetuous gestures, and if we had not been bound hand and foot by Regular Order we would likely have been making them all the time, prodigious feasts, bloody vigils, the whole catalog of Coptic excesses. We were spared the excesses of our own inflamed psyches by a tight and prescribed regimen which allowed no place for personal statements, pious or otherwise. But if one really craved self-immolation, he could always sit down and write to the Provincial volunteering for the missions. It did not mean that you would be sent, and yet the odds were sufficiently unattractive that I never wrote that letter. But the impeccable George Flattery, that soft and elegant creature, had and was being sent to some remote South Pacific atoll to spend the rest of his life swatting mosquitoes and trying to convert the Trukese to Catholicism.

Like all such pregnant events, George's departure for the Carolines was deeply masticated by the Novices until they had extracted the last savory morsel of moral marrow from the bones. It was a triumph for the moral sages who maintained that they always knew that the Father Rector was *solid,* even though he celebrated Mass at the high altar wearing what very much appeared to be black patent-leather loafers. How else could he have become a Rector, they argued, if he wasn't *solid?* The worldly-wise didn't even deign to respond to that patently fallacious piece of logic; they were more likely imagining

George Flattery sitting tanned and relaxed in an outrigger canoe, his custom-tailored white cassock gleaming like snow against the blue Pacific, while fifty chanting Micronesian maidens paddled his royal barque. Never mind, you cynics, it was still an astonishing and edifying piece of news.

After George Flattery departed to his remote apostolate, he was replaced at the high altar by an equally unlikely figure. Father John Hudson, S.J., was small and lumpy and had a funny mincing walk. He was very soft and white and spoke so quietly as to be inaudible. He looked incalculable and so possibly dangerous. It was no matter at present. What did matter for the Novices was that he said the community Mass, even with some two hundred communicants, in something under thirty-five minutes. Which meant that we knelt there in chapel for nearly thirty more minutes before breakfast with nothing else to contemplate but a too familiar stained-glass window and the ruins of our earlier meditation. John Hudson too became a legend: he had singlehandedly managed to add a half hour to our morning meditation.

We did not spend a great deal of time in that chapel. One of the more civilized aspects of Jesuit life was that it was relatively free, even in the Novitiate, of mindless little devotional exercises. All Jesuits either heard or said Mass daily, and the Fathers had privately to read their Daily Office, the prayers prescribed for all priests. But while the monastic orders were night and day plain-chanting their way through vespers and nones and such, the only devotion the entire Jesuit community shared in common was the nightly litanies in the chapel, which took only about fifteen minutes, depending on the alacrity and compassion of the Father who was reading them. Novices were Novices, however, and one small devotional thorn was inserted in our inexpert flesh so we could more deeply savor the pleasure of its removal. It was called "Prayers."

Every day after noon recreation we collected in the chapel where the Manuductor led us on a dusty and pointless voyage of twenty minutes through that vapid miscellany of orisons. What Prayers were all about or where they had come from no one who had addressed the question quite understood. My best guess is that they were begun by some pious turkey back in the primeval ooze of Jesuit Novitiates, had taken on the aura of tradition because no one was looking, and now ruined my afternoons. Or perhaps they were just dropped into an empty time slot to make trial of our collective patience.

The Novitiate was filled with tests of our virtue and adaptability, constant and random changes in our work assignments, desks, beds, admonitors and even companions at recreation. But the Rules prescribed as well somewhat more formal trials for the Novices, certain drastic changes of condition to see how we would fare on our own. "Drastic" is perhaps too strong a word. The only thing drastic about the Novitiate was leaving it, and so we had no expectations of being shipped down to make trial of a weekend at the Plaza. Instead we were sent off in threes to live with the Lay Brother Novices for two weeks. We took our pitiful gear down to the other end of the long hall and entered the Other Caste. We lived in their tiny ascetory and dormitory, ate with them in the refectory, knelt with them in the chapel, recreated with them and worked at their tasks. Their formation as Novices was a little "softer" and less structured than what we were accustomed to, but it was obviously cut from the same Jesuit cloth.

Lay Brothers were, however, different people. They entered the Jesuits generally at an older age with less and a different education and were headed for a different life. We were going to be mandarin priests; they, mechanics and cooks and bookkeepers; all of us, Jesuits. The eight Lay Brother Novices whom I joined were apparently simpler and certainly less cynical people than the Scholastic Novices I had left. I tried to respond, to avoid corrupting what seemed to me like innocence. For their part, they had no obvious reaction to us or to the caste system that had put such an abyss between us.

Recreation with them was a curious affair. They did not talk and I listen; rather I questioned them as endlessly and closely as if they had been transsexuals or Martians. What was it *really* like to be a Lay Brother? Theirs seemed so different from our own life as Scholastics. Like us, they had a two-year Novitiate in that same house, but once it was over, they took up the tasks that would engage them for the rest of their Jesuit lives, while we had before us another thirteen years of training.

There was something slightly demeaning in the term "Lay Brother," I always thought. In Latin they were more forthrightly called *coadjutores*, "fellow workers," and that is what they were. They took vows like all Jesuits; they were "religious" as surely as we were. The

United States is filled with religious orders whose entire membership is made up of Brothers, nonpriests. The problem for Jesuit Brothers is that they had joined a society where they were a small minority and whose primary work was so relentlessly intellectual that they could not in effect share in it to any real degree. No, despite my questions I could not crawl into their skin, and after this brief visit to their world I would go my own way, and they theirs. I esteemed them, but I'm not sure my esteem was totally without condescension.

As fictive Lay Brother Novices we worked for and with the Professed Lay Brothers—"professed" in Jesuit jargon meant that you had completed your training, whether Father or Brother, and had taken your final vows. They were a very mixed lot, probably because they had come from a far wider range of backgrounds than the Scholastics and the Fathers: the lovely and gracious Brother Czajka who supervised the kitchen with immense calm and tranquility; his assistant, the elderly and garrulous German, Brother Heer; the dim and cloddish Brother Adel who ran the chicken farm and defiantly came to dinner with dung-covered boots under his cassock and a heavy but knowing smile on his face; Brother J. O'Brien, the worldly-wise baker; Brother Garvin, the large Florence Nightingale of the shell-shocked Novices; Brother Walzer, an exotic and enigmatic figure who was sacristan and who played the chapel organ in a manner that imparted a ludicrous air to even the most sacred of canticles; Brother Dooley, the Brother Porter who worked the various visitors' facilities outside the cloister; Brother Paul Kerr, a gross and slightly unsavory operator of immense girth who was Brother Buyer, or purchasing agent, for the house and who spent more time between Poughkeepsie and New York City than in the cloisters of St. Andrew.

It was an oddly relaxing two weeks, one of them in the sacristy, where I spent most of my time buffing the wooden floor of the sanctuary to an unnatural glow; and a week with Brother Dooley at the Front Door, that window on the World where Novices and Juniors received their visitors and where secular retreatants were occasionally lodged. Other people's visitors all looked pretty much alike, all except their younger sisters, my putative companions of that Other Life. Brother Brennan's sister was the Irish fulfillment of every one of my inconclusive fantasies, and Brother Watson's family appeared to consist of nothing else but extremely attractive young ladies of a type I thought I had never experienced before. Nor had I, in fact. Brother Watson came from the very rich Catholic aristocracy. In our midst he was just another Novice, but outside the cloister, in the guests' dining room and on the lawns of St. Andrew, his social class reflected back on his anonymous cassock from the brightly polished faces of the Watson girls.

Brother Dooley, who was in his fifties, appeared to be quite immune to the brilliant young Scholastic recruit who was to be his assistant for a week. He looked sophisticated, as I then read sophistication, but he said little, and so I was left to dust the floors and the halls and to construct the bases of his sophistication in any way I chose. It was by no means a simple task. The Scholastic Novices were all fresh from high school and from almost identical middle-class Irish Catholic backgrounds. Where Brother Dooley or Brother Czajka came from, or when, could not even be imagined. Brother Rafferty, it was rumored, had been married and widowed before he entered the Society and took up the supervision of the heating plant at St. Andrew. But who *really* knew? Discussing the worldly past was not considered very good form, and particularly with Lay Brothers, who were to be permitted their privacy, probably on the assumption that they were the only ones who had a worldly past.

Two weeks as a Lay Brother Novice was interesting, but there was a far more exotic surprise in store. One of the prescribed trials for Novices was some kind of service outside the house. That sounded more like a treat than a trial, and so when it was announced during my second year that this particular trial was to be reinstituted after long disuse, the news sent shock waves of anticipation through our highly inflammable body. Even when it was revealed that the service would take the form of two weeks of housework at the Tertianship in Auriesville, New York, it still sounded like reclining on the bosom of Thaïs for a spell, one of the favorite pastimes of Rodríguez' Desert Fathers—before their conversion, that is.

The Tertianship was the final stage of the Jesuit course, an unbelievable third year of Novitiate for the sophisticates who thought they had seen everything, and Auriesville was the perfect setting for this perverse enterprise. The Tertian Fathers were housed in a nasty functional building, which was the only living part of a large and desolate tract along the Mohawk River that bore the grandiose and ironic name of the Shrine of the North American Martyrs. The present Tertians apart, there had been Jesuit martyrs galore in that Mohawk vale, but the spiritual spotlight rested unmistakably upon the Venerable Kateri Tekakwitha, an Iroquois maiden who had been converted to Christianity by seventeenth-century Jesuit missionaries and died warding off an attack on her virginity by certain of her misapprised contemporaries.

It had once been hoped that Ms. Tekakwitha would take off from this spectacular flaunting of local custom and make it to the heights of canonization ahead of the other candidates for the title of First American Saint. But she had stubbornly refused to produce the requisite miracle, and even then it was clear that she was not going to make it.* And so this failed Lourdes with its mournful bark benches and birchwood kiosks echoed only to the halfhearted cries of young Jesuit priests doing their softball exercises one last time before taking up their apostolic ministry.

Our "trial" took place not in the Tertianship itself but in a small retreat house that the Jesuits ran for diocesan priests on the same property. We were shipped up there three at a time, put like mail on a train at Poughkeepsie and retrieved by the retreat master at Fonda, New York. The trip was filled with unrequited curiosity. This was

---

*In formal ceremonies held in the Vatican on June 22, 1980, Kateri Tekakwitha was solemnly promoted from the status of "Venerable" to that of "Blessed." The Blessed Kateri still has a long way to go to sainthood.

my first day or night out of St. Andrew in over a year, and I longed to see or experience something interesting, some faint, blandishing melody from the World. There is little of the World between Poughkeepsie and Fonda-Auriesville and none at all at the Shrine of the North American Martyrs. We never even laid eyes on a Tertian, those Grand Masters of the Course who presumably had wisdom, or at least some baseball scores, to impart. We were equally remote from the seven or eight diocesan priests, who were, after all, on silent retreat, and from the retreat director, who had other, unseen ways of amusing himself than by conversing with three second-year Novices.

So we were alone, Brothers Gilligan, LaBella and I, in a miniature Novitiate suspended in outer space beyond reach of the Manuductor and the Master of Novices. We meditated, heard Mass, set up and cleaned up before and after the priests' meals, cared for the house and took our recreation on three wicker rockers on a porch overlooking the dour Mohawk. We were a kind of Eternal Band, chained to each other's company without relief for two weeks. We explored the shrine with its pathetic rustic Stations of the Cross, but mostly we rocked on that porch and told North American Martyr jokes. The final vicious assault on the Venerable Kateri was neither discussed nor meditated.

Two other sets of Novices had gone through the Auriesville experience before we arrived. The first three, Brothers Braun, Cloney and McGarry, were all extremely solid, since they were going to establish the new Regular

Order of this unique enterprise and commit it to the Diary, which would be the governing charter of our lives for two weeks. It was a harmless code, as it turned out, with a great deal of space for improvisation. Someone had already improvised, it seemed, since there in an earlier entry were the words "Tonight, after recreation, began the Perpetual Novena to the North American Martyrs."

It was a revelation. There before my eyes was tradition in the making; it was like being present at the birth of Prayers. It also galled. Some mindless innovator had simply decided out of the depths of his own piety to start something that would chain a thousand years of Novices. He was not very good at it. A shrewder hand would have omitted the "tonight began" and have passed up the pleading urgency of "perpetual."

It was a time for decision. This tradition was only three weeks old and so still vulnerable. Chuck Gilligan was all for a mortal blow; novenas did not much engage his interest. Brother LaBella was mulch for traditions, however, since they were supported by unseen authority and he, like the rest of us, had a healthy fear of authority, seen or unseen. It was really up to me. I both disliked novenas and feared the consequences of killing one in cold blood. But the temptation to traditicide was too great. With the grateful cries of unborn Novices ringing in my ears, I wrote in the Diary: "Tonight, after recreation, ended the Perpetual Novena to the North American Martyrs." Maybe the Master would think that Chuck had written it. Sure.

VI

Spiritual Theater

1. BROTHER GELLER IN CHAINS

When fascination with Aloysius Gonzaga grew thin, there was always Brother Geller. Some Novices lived in an unmarked penumbra for two years; others stood forth only at the full moon or under the bright sunlight of some spectacular, attention-getting event. But there was no overlooking Brother Geller: each new Novice noticed him within the first five minutes after his arrival and never took his eyes off him thereafter. He had an unaccountable, soft-gaunt face that exuded a quite alarming sweetness. Simultaneously his eyes were cast modestly downward and gloriously heavenward in some way I still cannot fathom. And his body—the word is too bold: whatever it was that Brother Geller had under his cassock—was contorted into piety.

As Rodríguez was constantly instructing us, holy men

are reputed to give off a special aroma, the odor of piety, which betokens their inner holiness. Brother Geller emitted no smell; rather, he had assumed, walking, sitting or kneeling, the *posture* of sanctity. It was grace, sanctifying grace, under the pressure of an ungainly and unwanted flesh. Possessed of this unsolicited physical burden of a body, Brother Geller contrived to make it look uncomfortable at all times. All except his head. That was in repose, slightly tilted to the side in the manner that the unwritten tradition dictated for pious carriage of the skull.

Brother Geller smiled with his eyes closed. No one mistook it for a chuckle over some inner joke, some previously hidden irony he had detected in that irony-filled landscape. Rather, it was thought to be a response to some interior spiritual concert, some presentiment of the angelic choirs. No one asked him, of course, what he found so amusing. Brother Geller neither gave nor invited confidences; he floated by on a great sea of holy oblivion.

For the rest of us Brother Geller posed spiritual problems of the most basic sort. Here was somebody who had apparently reached the stage of perfection toward which we were all so manfully striving. There he was, totally observant, totally sanctified and totally, existentially offputting. Brother Geller was not a simple shit—he was far too passive to be really noisome—but he was distinctly, well, unappetizing. He made the flesh crawl and the heart sink. Sanctity, the Master soothingly intoned, was infinitely appealing, and then the eye fell upon Brother Geller, a living refutation of that proposition. Is that what we were supposed to be like? There was no answer, of course, for the simple reason that no one would conceivably pose that question to the Master. But it did give an interesting contemporary perspective on old Aloysius Gonzaga, S.J.

Which is not to say that Brother Geller was useless. He was terrific for exercising charity toward. And when one or other of us got our inevitable dose of consolation, some little nuance of Gellerism could be mimed to put flesh on our newfound piety. We all knew how to *act* holy—a perfect observance of the Rule would do as a starter—but no one knew how to *appear* holy. What does piety look like? It looked like Brother Geller, obviously, and if few were willing or able to don the entire sackcloth of his persona, small essays of Geller gait, bearing and, for the heroic, converse could be undertaken. The ambidextrous eyes were difficult to manage perhaps, but the tilt of the head and the silent smile both had their occasional fanciers, while Brother Geller at meals provided more advanced dramatic material for the truly venturesome.

Tuesdays and Thursdays were virtuoso Geller days. We rose, donned our chains and strode, with perfect mastery of our tortured limbs—playing through pain, it was later to be called—through the early duties of the day. But not Brother Geller. Though his face was as appallingly beatific as ever, he dragged his leg as if it were afflicted with gangrene. Brother Geller limped! And not modestly, but outrageously! It was a terrifying spectacle because it was the only part of the Geller performance that didn't make sense. He lived by the book and his own perverse lights; he *was* extravagant, but he did not indulge in them. In the best Jesuit style he did not pray longer than others (his life was a prayer, I know, I know); he did not fast more severely than custom permitted. But his matutinal limp was patently extravagant.

The simple preferred the vulgar opinion, of course. Brother Geller, it was professed, wore the chain as tightly as human endurance permitted. Witness: if some merely mortal pressure made the rest of us incline toward the oblique, Brother Geller's chain must be like a veritable Gonzagan tourniquet; his withered thigh must be all but bloodily severed to hobble such a pro. That theorem was for children and fools. Brother Geller *was* a pro. That was the point. To test his already superb obedience, I posited, the Master had privately *forbidden* Brother Geller to wear the chain, no matter how much his heroic soul lusted after such self-affliction. His limping but unfettered leg was, then, a master performance in the Theater of Humility. He appeared to wear the chain like the rest of us, but he also gave the impression that *he couldn't handle it!* A stroke of genius pure and simple, but not to those of us who were on to him.

2. HOLIDAYS ABROAD

The liturgical calendar is far more lavish with holidays than its secular counterpart. A profusion of saints' days— mostly Jesuit saints, to be sure—and the octaves of great Church feasts stretched across the year, bringing to the Novices at least temporary respite from Regular Order. As the occasion dictated, there were lucullan dinners in the refectory or a variety of outings to unappetizing places.

The outings took different forms, but the most curious was surely the walk called *ambulatio in bonis vestimentis*. The "good clothes" in question were not the black suits that we had been commanded to bring with us—they were reserved for the true clerical state that would follow upon vows—but those innocuous high-school suits in which we had presented ourselves as candidates. As we emerged from the house for this occasional Sunday exercise, it was an odd experience to regard each other once again in our former worldly vestments. All black-robed anonymity was suddenly shed, and visions of earlier lives, earlier by only a few months or a year, rose up like ghosts from the past. There were few surprises, however. The cassocked wise-ass predictably appeared in a one-button lounge suit of a once fashionable rust color. The boring had boring Staten Island clothes. And the pious, it turned out, had worn dark and pious suits even in high school. You wear what you are. And to make sure *that* was understood, we all sported black fedoras.

We wore these now strange clothes because this particular walk took us outside the grounds onto the back roads of Dutchess County. We had no particular destination; we just walked for two hours or so past indifferent cows and apparently deserted farmhouses. Over the years the good burghers of Dutchess may have become accustomed to this bizarre sight: bands of three young men in business suits and black fedoras walking purposefully—everything was to be done purposefully, even though the purpose might elude merely human understanding—through the middle of nowhere. Or perhaps they superstitiously took refuge behind locked doors and closed shutters during those rambles.

I am not a big fan of walking, purposeful or otherwise, though the thought of a couple of hours of uninterrupted talk was attractive. If only we could have sat down somewhere. Unthinkable. *Ambulatio* meant walking, and walk we did. And lest the ambulation turn into an orgy of self-indulgence, we always walked in assigned bands. Randomness deserted me: on two of the first four occasions I was committed with a partner to the senior care of Brother O'Connell. Brother O'Connell was very tall, and rumors that he could handle a basketball had already whetted Brother Gilligan's appetite for some matchups in a basketball game still a year and a half away. Chuck Gilligan could live on such fantasy perhaps, but meanwhile I had to parade through Dutchess County with the long-striding and apparently indefatigable Brother Francis O'Connell.

Brother O'Connell was a lousy conversationalist, or perhaps an ideal one by Novitiate standards, since in his company there was no gossip and no talk of the World, even under the transparent ploy of contemning it. After Brother O'Connell's commitment to pious converse was established, there was only one remaining tactic, to attempt to talk across him to my contemporary at his other elbow. Brother O'Connell was always boring but only fitfully dim, and when he realized that he was losing control of the conversational ball, he simply went into a full-court press in the shameless and unembarrassed manner of the pious and proceeded to discourse sweetly on God's blessing in giving us such a good day, or, if it were raining pestilentially, how Divine Providence . . .

The quintessential outing was the boat ride. When the *Normandy* was scrapped, the Jesuits bought the outsize lifeboats of that transatlantic liner to serve as pleasure craft and carry Novices and Juniors on summer excursions a few miles up the Hudson to the island of Esopus. This latter was an island only in the sense that it had unaccountably risen from beneath the Hudson River. It was actually a pile of rock with no trees attached, a Caucasus landscape right out of *Prometheus Bound*. Happily there was not even room to walk a good rosary on its stony sides.

There was room to eat, however, and that seemed the chief point of this endless and tiring entertainment. Jesuits did not picnic like other people; no ham sandwiches or warm potato salad for them. We young ascetics feasted instead on a vast quantity of French toast entirely concealed by an equally vast field of ice cream. For dessert we sat on the rocky ribs of Esopus, contemplated the Marist Brothers Novitiate on the distant shore and thanked God that we were not Marist Brothers.

But first we had to get there, and in those lifeboats. Craft they assuredly were, though built more for sturdiness in the North Atlantic than for skimming the pacific Hudson. What the pleasure consisted of was more obscure. Those monsters seated about forty souls around the gunwales. Down the length of the keel ran a screw shaft straddled by thirty more Novices seated two by two on benches and heaving to and fro on handles that turned the shaft. Every half hour or so the gunwale squatters replaced the lifeless handle-pullers in the keel pit. In the originally foreseen circumstances help would presumably arrive to save the frightened passengers of the *Normandy* from death by exhaustion. No help ever arrived for the

Stella Maris, as every Catholic boat is inevitably named. Deserted by all but the angels, who never pull their own weight, we screwed away against the inexorable Hudson tide.

One hot morning we had gotten about halfway to Esopus when even the screw had had enough. We stopped dead in our wake and then began to drift slowly southward. The boats were in the charge of responsible people, a changeable concept, but in this case two soberly pious young men who also knew something about machines. They were both from Buffalo, where both responsibility and the machine had been invented, it was said. Our captain was Brother Vogelsinger. He was "older"—whatever that word meant at that time and place; he could have been anywhere from twenty-five to seventy-eight—and he was assuredly sober. Rumor had it that he had been an undertaker, a report about as reliable as his purported age. And his name was obviously fair game to seventy kids, most of whom were named O'Brien.

The rowers sat frozen to their handles, momentarily gratified by the respite, while Brother Vogelsinger handed the tiller to the nearest Buffalo Novice and opened the gear box. When some incident like this occurred, the reaction was highly predictable. Most thought nothing: they chatted comfortably about the foliage on the now rapidly gliding banks of the Hudson; whatever was the matter, Vogelsinger would fix it. A tiny minority, Brother Geller at their head, filed it under God's plan and meditated it under that pious rubric. Another minority, though somewhat larger than the first, had another file at hand. It was labeled TARBO, an acronym doubtless borrowed from some similar but obscene wartime usage but meaning here "Typical Affair Run By Ours." A TARBO was also God's plan, but one calculated to entertain as well as instruct by shoving the vanities of human purpose up the noses of the innocent. It was in fact an insight into Murphy's Law well before the formulation of that cosmic rule.

The Master knew perfectly well that TARBO was an essentially subversive concept, and without so much as mentioning the forbidden acronym he had made it clear on many occasions that it was neither an adequate nor an appropriate explanation of anything. It was not uttered now either, but a large number of people seated in the slowly drifting *Stella Maris* had a large and radiant "T" glowing like stigmata upon their impassive brows.

Brother O'Leary made the first really practical suggestion.

"Dingledanger, if you just leave the gears alone, we'll drift all the way to New York."

O'Leary was instantly enshrined in the Novice Hall of Fame. No one had thought of that unlikely but interesting possibility.

"Finglesinger, have you ever conducted a burial at sea?"

"Is the food in the other boat?"

"It's all right. We can pick some up in New York."

"Whatever happened to the *Normandy*, Bingleslinger?"

Brother Vogelsinger had had enough. The gear box was dirty, hot and unyielding to his ministrations and/or prayers. And the troops were getting out of control.

"I declare Sacred Silence."

There were, in the best Talmudic fashion, two kinds of

silences in the Novitiate. Your normal, garden-variety silence prevailed at all times except for recreation. It was not absolute and you could obviously ask questions and give commands as necessity dictated and your Latin permitted. The other was Sacred Silence. It was in force from lights out until after Mass in the morning, and it brooked no exceptions. It also surfaced in another interesting context, however. In summer we swam on occasion in a natural pool formed by a frigid stream on the property. We changed into our bathing suits in a small and thin stand of trees next to the pool, and Sacred Silence was in force for as long as we were in that grove. Nude chitchat was clearly an unacceptable form of social intercourse.

When Brother Vogelsinger proclaimed Sacred Silence as we sat in mid-Hudson at high noon with all our clothes on, he got silence, though not of the sacred variety. We were all pondering the grave question he had raised. Was Sacred Silence, and God knows what else, part of a divinely ordained natural order or an enactment by a mere human agent, perhaps even Brother Vogelsinger? The silent vote took no more than thirty seconds and then the *Stella Maris* erupted with laughter. And talk. Something important had happened out there on the river. The Emperor had loaned his clothes to Brother Vogelsinger, and poor old Wanglewringer was assuredly naked.

3. LUDI VEL LABORANDUM

The front of the Jesuit house had a neatly kept lawn that sloped gracefully toward the river. Calm and tranquility reigned over this manicured sward, the silence broken only by the soft and sweet chatter of family visitors who could come up the Hudson on three or four Sundays a year and sit and chat a spell with their Novice son or brother. Behind the house, however, other sounds and other moods prevailed. There were our playgrounds: handball, tennis and basketball courts and a softball field.

The Novitiate experience was unabashedly constructed upon calculated privations. If there had been a special Jesuit language with a vocabulary of only ten words, the Novices would have been constrained to conduct their business in five of those vocables chosen randomly out of the entire set. There was, in fact, a special Jesuit language. It was called sports, and the Novices were inevitably forbidden to play with a full deck. The Juniors might engage in whatever sport they would; the Novices were confined, without rhyme or any visible reason, to softball and handball. In the Novitiate, as in Heaven, one didn't have to supply reasons to us perfect fans of perfect obedience.

The naive Extern might cluck approvingly over our little sportive exercises and pronounce it a capital idea that the youngsters should have lots of fresh air and exercise. And I suppose it was. But to confuse what we did out there on those playing fields with exercise would be tantamount to thinking that the Pittsburgh Steelers were putting on their pads to go out and have some fun with a pigskin. No, we had something else in mind besides exercise. For some, it was a grueling ordeal; for others, a veritable debauch.

Novitiate life had its terrors, numbered and unnumbered, but one of the most terrible must have been the fatal choices forced upon the uncoordinated, the uncompetitive and the effeminate, those high-school kids who for one reason or another did not care about sports. But the explicit tradition of The Life was that you *had*, at one time or another, to do everything, and an even larger part of the unspoken ethos was that sports were as good a way as any to relieve young males of their physical—read erotic—energies.

To fill the letter of the law, the athletically inept generally chose to play handball, where they would be safely out of the way of the vicious samurai who were bloodying talon and claw on each other's person on the softball field. Many of them descended, even within the modest handball galaxy, to the feeble asteroid called paddleball, which, by enlarging both the ball and the hand, increased the odds of making some kind of contact and so constituting a game. The paddleball players didn't really care whether they made contact or even generated a score. They were "playing," as was prescribed for that time and that place, and that was enough. *Nemo dat quod non habet*, "Nobody gives what he doesn't possess," was a favorite Novitiate aphorism, and its truth was illustrated every Thursday afternoon between two and four on the handball courts of St. Andrew on Hudson.

Thursdays and Sundays were our holidays, when the ordinary work assignments were suspended and other, more tantalizing dishes were put before the Novices. Sundays were generally peaceful affairs, and a common form of Sunday afternoon recreation was the walk, in the inevitable bands of three, around the hundreds of wooded acres within our Jesuit reservation, or the occasional *ambulatio in bonis vestimentis* across a startled Dutchess County. But Thursday was different. The daily order posted for that day put it to us direct: *Ludi vel laborandum.* Sports *or* work. The choice was ours, the dulcet *ludi* or the ominously gerundive *laborandum.*

Let's see, what do I feel like doing this Thursday? That innocuous thought never, I am sure, entered a single Novice head. Choices were not offered to Jesuits to cater to their whims or fancies. Rather, they were proffered like a little spiritual whetstone upon which one could hone one's self-denial to such a fine edge that it could cut the World in half. If there was any exercise in our Thursday sports, it was there, in the choice of whether one would go out and frolic under the sun or whether one would give the Self a good thrashing under the guise of *laborandum.* There it was, another Thursday, another chance to graze with the sanctified sheep or gambol with the smelly goats.

The sheep didn't exactly graze; *laborandum* was more like a season in Hell. On went the heavy boots, the army surplus pants and jacket. You shouldered something called a mattock and headed, together with the others who had chosen well, into the Ardennes of the soul. I had never even heard of a mattock before I went through those sacred portals. It had an ax handle, but the head was on one side an unpointed pick and on the other an unsharpened blade. It was an instrument for inhuman activity—hacking. Hacking at stone, if you were fatally deranged, or, as often there, at fallen trees and brush. It was not effective, it was not satisfying, and it certainly was not fun. It was perfect *laborandum*.

The Master believed in the hearty outdoor life that seemed to characterize most of downtown Buffalo. He also believed in underlining choices for the dim-witted. So every Thursday afternoon he stood outside the back door in *his* boots, pants and jacket, and awaited those Novices who had made the virtuous sheeplike choice of clearing the woods. He held no mattock in his hand, however; he had a sharp and shiny ax, something even more remote and forbidden to the Novice than a basketball. The Master was known to hand that bright and dangerous blade to a very experienced (and *solid*) Novice to take a few whacks on occasion. As in all such cases, it was assumed he had his reasons and no one even dared aspire to such high favor.

Or so I speculated. In the hundred-odd Thursdays I spent as a Novice, I never once chose *laborandum*. That was not, perhaps, playing the game; or, rather, it was playing quite another game. The sportive goats no more gamboled on the softball field than their sheepish brethren grazed in the terrible woods. Ours were not lazy, summer afternoon outings redolent of root beer and the quiet thud of bat upon ball. Waterloo may indeed have been won years earlier on the playing fields of Eton. The more economical Novices simply fought their Waterloo *at* Eton. Every ounce of suppressed adolescent hostility, every homicidal design and Hunnish impulse to rapine and destruction was released on that softball field and later, when we were Juniors, on the basketball court. We were turned out of our cages and for two hours we could commit sublimated rape, murder and mayhem. For those who chose *ludi,* Thursday afternoons were like Mardi Gras.

After lunch and an ambulatory rosary said in bands of three, the *ludi* types collected at the softball field. By a secret but swift process—time was at a premium here—two were made captains and chose their teams by alternating selections from the pool of players, just as they had in the World. And the World's rules prevailed: the strong, the skilled and the competitive were chosen first; the others, those slumming a little in their search for perfect self-denial, followed in descending order of desirability and were assigned to innocuous positions like right field where they were permitted to play but were expected to have the good sense not to interfere with the point of the game, which was to win.

Good spirits prevailed for an inning or two or until we reached the nether part of the batting order when, by the inflexible rules of our National Pastime, the inept had to be permitted to bat. Balls whizzed perilously close to feckless heads. There were near-fatal collisions at all bases—the wisdom of not permitting football was patent—and the desire to win slowly came to a boil, painfully unvented by even the slightest obscenity. Softball may have been invented as a sport, but the Novices played it like Miltonic warfare on a darkling plain.

No one of our company understood that better than Brother Charles Gilligan, N.S.J., no one perhaps in the entire history of the Society of Jesus. Chuck played everything in high school. He was smallish then and not very skillful, but he was totally committed to playing and winning. At sixteen he had the perfectly formed psyche of a jock; at nineteen Jesuit food and Jesuit sleep had given him a body which, if it was not the graceful instrument of the true athlete, was large enough and powerful enough to give a bloody conviction to his playing. Playing? Chuck did not play, of course; he was in this war for keeps. He kept personal statistics on every game he was ever in. His wore his sneakers to lunch on Thursdays, his fatigues under his cassock.

Chuck was the kind of person you avoided, every time, everywhere, in free bands and foul. Except when sides were being chosen on the softball field. He was loud and coarse. The evidence was powerful that he never washed, and so it was predictable that as a Novice Brother Gilligan contracted that mysterious disease known as "the crud." I had never heard of the crud before my Jesuit days, but it was real enough in the Novitiate, a kind of prodigious athlete's foot of the body. And it was regarded as one of the more extravagant proofs not only for the existence of God but for His unrelenting justice that Chuck contracted one of the most virulent cases of the crud known to medical annals.

The only known cure for the crud, if not for Chuck, was to cover the reluctant patient from head to toe with a kind of calamine lotion. Chuck was removed to the infirmary, where he tossed vilely in his own filth, and I was assigned to supply him with reading matter from the house library. He ate books, possibly because he was trying for some obscure world record. I fed him history in immense gulps. He devoured the Jesuits, their works and pomps, as a starter, took all of English history in a couple of unchewed mouthfuls, and was well into the Civil War before God restored him to the playing fields. I carried all the generously calamined books back to the library, where they must have puzzled, and possibly infected, an entire generation of readers.

It was the only part of any season that Brother Gilligan ever missed. He suffered no groin or muscle pulls, no hip-pointers or other newfangled injuries. On Thursday afternoons he stood impatiently outside the back door swinging a few bats and waiting for those who improvidently had to change their clothes. When he said a rosary before a softball game, he defied, even by the somewhat lax Jesuit standards, every liturgical canon known to Christendom. "Yeah," said Chuck after a particularly satisfying rosary, "broke seven minutes today." It was well known that he inspected the infield playing surface during his prayerful march, and that by the time the last Hail Mary had flown from his lips he had already checked out the day's player personnel for draft choices.

The Chucker and the other fanciers of the sport were already assembled and choosing sides when the Master and his dour band of hackers rosaried past on their way to the woods. We started at 2 P.M. and we were expected to be re-collected and recollected at the back door at four when the chapel bell sounded the end of recreation. The Master sometimes brought his sheep home early to give them a head start on the showers and unwittingly teach them the timeless lesson that virtue is not entirely its own reward. The shower edge tempted no one from *ludi* to *laborandum*, of course, and certainly not Chuck, who thought the constant references to showers had to do with the weather.

On occasion the Master showed his own superb self-denial by releasing his troops early to the showers and requesting a turn in the hateful softball game. He was an indifferent player: no speed, no power, mediocre hands. Chuck had scouted him early on and pronounced the Reverend Grissom incapable of handling a curve tight inside on the hands. Maybe so. But I doubt if he factored in the all-important "attitude." The Master did not care about winning. He too did not regard softball as a game. For him it was an opportunity to work up a sweat, to exert yourself; it was not playing through pain but paining through play. It was enough to make Chuck retch.

"Who's the captain here, Brother?"

"Brother Gilligan, Father."

Slight frown, slight controlled smile. The Master is forced to avert to the fact that Chuck had chosen *ludi* again. I try to disappear in the outfield grass.

"Do you have a place for me, Brother Gilligan?" the Master asks ever so quietly.

"Sure, Father." The Chucker is already revising his batting order for the next inning. "Why don't you play shortstop."

Craven Chuck. The Master loved to play shortstop, where he could pepper the action and keep the game "moving," as he understood that term. He trots briskly out to his position, which Brother Navins quietly vacates for short-center-left field.

"Let's play some ball here," quoth the Master from the

Book of Life. Chuck obliges in the only way he knows how, by sending the next batter sprawling into the dirt. Another magisterial frown.

On the way back to the house I told Chuck he was a coward for yielding the Master shortstop.

"Oh yeah?" he retorted in his usual sophisticated way.

I have my own shot at Father Big soon enough. Another Thursday, another game.

"Do you have a place for me, Brother?"

Let him look. It really is a choice, isn't it? Isn't that what *vel* means? And do I have a place for you!

"Let's see." A dramatic pause to suggest reflection. "Why don't you play right field, Father?"

Silence under the sun. The Master of Novices sent to right field, the graveyard, the haunt of faggots and sissies. A different kind of frown and a different smile. A triumph becomes a rout: the Master heads for the showers right after the third out. Not even a time at bat. He *can* be had, and not only by an inside curve! As the Master disappears toward the house, no word is spoken. The game proceeds silently, even solemnly. Not even Chuck wants to dilute the immense satisfaction of one of our own striking out the Master of Novices.

4. FIRST-CLASS RELIC

We had, for our pains, occasional unscheduled entertainments. For weeks we reveled in the Affair Father Feeney. We all knew who Father Feeney was. Every high-school student fed on four Jesuit authors: the Reverend

Robert Gannon, S.J., who delivered reputedly witty after-dinner speeches which, when they were written down, turned into essays of the purest dross; the Reverend Daniel Lord, S.J., who instructed Catholic teenagers on how love could pass directly to parenthood without once touching down filthy foot on the terrain marked "sex"; the Reverend Robert Henle, S.J., who composed an impressive and widely read comic *oeuvre* entitled *Latin I, Latin II, Latin III* and the climactic *Latin IV;* and the Reverend Leonard Feeney, S.J., who wrote in that now extinct genre called "boys' stories."

Father Feeney had other strings in his bow, however. He had contrived to lead an entire conventicle of Harvard Catholics into, would you believe it, *schism.* We had only the vaguest idea what Harvard was, except that it was morbidly secular, like the YMCA or the Salvation Army, but we knew all about schism. And the thought that there was a Jesuit at the helm of a real schism was a source of perverse delight and a lot of cautionary tongue-clucking by those Novices who felt that there were in our midst others, like Brother Cole or Brother Hickman, not to mention names, who were probably headed in the same terrible direction.

The news from distant Cambridge filtered into the Novitiate through the same kind of mysterious osmosis that permitted Chuck Gilligan to keep up with the baseball standings. The osmotic process was not perfect, of course; no one knew what the precise schismatic issue was at Harvard, and it was well understood that Chuck frequently invented World Series scores when the going got thin. Most of the information probably came in with visitors to our cloister, parents and relatives and other Jesuits who came to St. Andrew to make their retreat and took their amusement in spreading tall tales in the febrile imagination of the Novices. We were astonished and delighted to hear, for example, that Clare Boothe Luce had converted Stalin to Catholicism on his deathbed and that Our Lady of Fatima had actually appeared on the floor of the U.S. Senate.

The Master never deigned to comment on any of this, of course, and no one ever dared inquire. We all *knew* the Feeney business was true—even the Lay Brothers confirmed it—but at the first scent of trouble the Reverend Leonard Feeney, S.J., had probably ceased to exist for the Reverend Robert Grissom, S.J., and not even a congenitally stupid Novice would have essayed broaching the subject. But the Master was human after all. Once in a very expansive mood he allowed that the Marian Year had opened in Rome. We all knew that had to be good news, even though none of us, even those highly regarded in Mariology, had the slightest clue as to what a Marian Year was. A few distractedly or wishfully thought they heard "Marrying Year," and it took two or three months to clear up *that* confusion.

All at once a new buzz was heard, and it grew into a roar until finally the Master gave it the official *imprimatur* at one of his conferences to the Novices. "The arm of Saint Francis Xavier is coming to St. Andrew. It will be a time of great blessings." An actual arm! Of an actual saint! We could scarcely wait to get to recreation and dissect this stunning piece of information and weigh its possible consequences for us. And, added the Magisteriologists, exactly gauge the Master's reaction to it. He seemed incapable of irony, that steely man, and yet the phrase "It will be a time of great blessings" had a most peculiar ring to it. Ancients of the First Probation searched their almost perfect memories and could come up with no recollection of ever having heard the Master utter it before.

Saint Francis Xavier, born 1506, died 1562 off the coast of China, was the greatest Jesuit missionary of them all, and if they had only listened to him in Rome he would have singlehandedly converted both India and Japan to Catholicism. His body, we all thought, was safely interred in the old Portuguese trading colony of Goa in south India. How his arm came to be separated from the rest of his torso no one professed to know, nor was it ever revealed in the sequel. But now, at any rate, it was heading toward us in a golden reliquary. Its acolyte on this improbable round-the-world trip was one Gerald Droghan, S.J. It was a little like entrusting the Holy Grail to P. T. Barnum. When Gerry Droghan appeared—the celebrated arm still well out of sight—it was immediately apparent that this enormous global boondoggle was *his* idea.

Our glamorous visitor was placed next to the Master the first night at dinner, with a couple of hundred pairs of beady Novice eyes boring straight into those hidden places in his being where the Droghan persona lay. It was not very well concealed. He sat there sleekly tailored and tonsured and smiling his showman's smile. We could not overhear the conversation, of course, but the Master's vein throbbed with Vesuvian disapproval. Whatever tale Gerry Droghan was spinning out with immense self-satisfaction for the Master's entertainment, it was assuredly not about Saint Francis Xavier. Nor was it much succeeding as entertainment.

The Novices were kept at a very safe distance from Gerald Droghan, S.J.; he would have undone the entire Long Retreat in a mere instant of converse. He appeared at dinner every night, always next to the Master, but no word ever passed between them in the blessed silence that reigned over most meals. Gerry turned instead to his distant Novice audience in the refectory. He beamed ingratiating smiles in our direction, nodded knowingly at the spiritual reading, leered at the waiters. But still no arm. We imagined heated debates between the Master and the Rector, the Master threatening to resign his office if Droghan ever appeared in public with that accursed member in his hands.

We may not have been very far wrong. Something had to be done; the uninvited arm of glorious Saint Francis Xavier could not be allowed to languish in a Jesuit Novitiate housed next to the underwear in the perfumed interior of Gerry Droghan's suitcase. A ceremony was arranged. Once the community was assembled, Droghan would bear the arm in procession from the rear of the chapel. But he would not do the honors. Within the sanctuary the reliquary would be surrendered into the sweetly innocent hands of a first-year Novice, who would hold it while the entire community approached two by two and reverenced this dismembered token of Jesuit sanctity with a kiss.

This was only a rough outline, as most Jesuit liturgical ceremonies in fact began and ended. The Jesuits did not much fancy the liturgy; it was not deemed worthy of a great deal of attention, even a trifle effete perhaps. The result was that most Jesuits had difficulty croaking and stumbling their way through anything more complicated than a Low Mass. Casual was the word, and casual was their attention to the details of this unprecedented liturgy for an arm. As was usually the case with unpleasant, unwonted or tedious affairs of the house, the exact arrangements were left in the hands of the Novice Sub.

The Sub usually did as he was bade, skimming off a little innocuous patronage and perk for himself and his friends. The present tenant of that office was Brother Neil, a bold and freckle-faced youth from Queens who had reputedly once spiked a lame and elderly Lay Brother in a close play at second base. While Brother Neil bethought his odd assignment, a less disinterested cabal bethought the very same thing with an intent that might charitably be called malicious. Droghan would be blown right out of his silk underwear, and if the shrapnel fell right, a few flesh wounds might be inflicted on the Master and a large number of entirely innocent bystanders.

It was assumed that Brother Neil could be had, that he would sacrifice his distinguished career in shoe repair for the opportunity to become a Novitiate legend. He would indeed, he grinned through his disarming freckles. The question was, who would be the engine of destruction, who was the most implausible Novice upon whom he might bestow the signal honor of holding hands with the Blessed F.X.? Chuck was, of course, the first candidate. No. Too common, too gross. Brother Geoghan perhaps, whose foul breath had in the space of five months rotted away two dozen pews in the chapel. An attractive idea, Brother Geoghan breathing upon the entire community, two by two. But we too would be of that number and no one was quite so fanatic as that. Brother Dromgool! Of course.

Brother Dromgool came to St. Andrew from either Brooklyn Prep or Outer Mongolia. Opinion was divided. He marched in our midst not to a different drummer but to an entire diverse orchestra that played tunes never heard by merely human ears. We all walked differently; Brother Dromgool existed differently, far out beyond the megahertz range of our feeble receivers. He could have been a mutant, the Father General of the Rosicrucians, a quicksilver betyl; he was assuredly not of our genus and species.

The Reverend Gerald Droghan, S.J., nattily attired in a starched white surplice—he could almost have passed for a cleric—preceded by a crossbearer and two candlebearers and followed by the Rector and the manifestly discomfited Master, swept majestically down the center aisle of the chapel, Xavier's golden-housed arm snuggled proprietarily in his own. In the sanctuary, flanked by two more candlebearers, stood Brother Dromgool, his filthy cassock gleaming dully in the flickering light. Even from a distance his eyes could be seen darting wildly behind his thick glasses. His lips twitched just this side of a full fit.

Droghan approached, all silvery in self-congratulation, and placed the reliquary in Brother Dromgool's now rigid arms. Yes, there it was. The Arm! Foolishly I had somehow imagined it in a black soutane, dressed, so to speak. What it actually was was a skeletal limb, and

Chuck was quick to note and draw the appropriate athletic conclusions from the unmistakable presence of bone chips in the elbow. My eyes narrowed on Droghan's piously inclined back. Was this *really* Xavier's arm?

We had all kissed relics before, tiny specks of indistinguishable matter behind glass in what appeared to be watch cases. A kneeling kiss, a quick swipe of a white handkerchief on the glass and then either you or the relic moved on. But this was no watch case; it was a three-foot-long golden torpedo with a glass side. Droghan knelt before Brother Dromgool and raised his foolish lips. Brother Dromgool failed to conceive. He held the case clutched tightly to his breast, well beyond the reach of even the most ardent lips, indeed, well over a foot above Droghan's head.

Droghan kept his wits. He stood, looked once and searchingly into Brother Dromgool's now madly twirling eyes and stood aside to bestow the honor of the first kiss upon the Rector and the Master. Fate and dignity conferred that privilege on the Rector, tiny John Hudson, kneeling just athwart Brother Dromgool's crotch. The reliquary was by now cradled up under the Dromgoolean chin. Neil, I thought, you're famous but you're finished. Wherever Brother Monahan is, you're going to be buried right next to him.

The Rector wisely decided to forgo his kiss, to substitute a simple bow of the head, very reverential, very rectorial, very improvised. The Master did not even kneel down. There was an ever so slight inclination of his head and he was down the aisle and out of the chapel trailing sparks of anger. Ours reveled in precedent, particularly when it saved you from the existential folly of attempting to kiss Francis Xavier in despite of Brother Dromgool. Two hundred souls marched up that aisle and nodded at Brother Dromgool. Brother Dromgool, ever alert, nodded back to each.

Ah, Brother Dromgool, where are you now? It was you and Geller and Vogelsinger and even the Chucker whose theatrics entertained and, I suppose, enlightened me through those twenty-four dark months. Larger than life they seemed, my fellow players, each struggling with his role as painfully as I in that morality play called the Novitiate. Each of us was presented an identical ideal of Jesuit sanctity, yet how different must have been the vision in each of our heads and how varied the response when confronted with the spiritual conundrums so skillfully built into the Jesuit life. Regular Order appeared the very antithesis of drama, and yet it presented to each of us tyro holy men matter that was as complex in its morality as it was banal in regard. On the Hudson or on the kneelers beside our desks, in the woods or the chapel or the dining hall, it was difficult to know whether to laugh or to cry. And though most of us kept a stoically straight face, the conviction was very strong that we should be doing one or the other when the casting director handed us our ever-changing parts.

VII

Deliverance

Novitiate time was like no other before or since. There were no calendars about and none of us had wristwatches, so time was a public rather than a private commodity. It was stored in large Seth Thomas clocks in the hall and the ascetory and dispensed to us in small particles by the Manuductor from his Ingersoll. It declared itself by bells, large chapel bells that tolled timeless metaphysical time, small ascetory bells that rang immediate, attention-getting, operational time. Time to go, to work, to meditate; time to sleep, to recreate, to pray.

What we were all counting off by toll or tinkle or tick was two years of Novitiate. Afterward I would have a wristwatch and keep my own private accounts, but for those twenty-four months we all swam together in time's river. The landmarks floated by on the shore: my first Christmas, first Lent, first Easter, easier days of the first summer, and then the reassuring but dispiriting spectacle of the second-year Novices taking their vows and their leave group by group in July, August and September and ascending majestically to the Juniorate.

Each group of blessed emigrants to the Holy Land was followed by the entry of new immigrants from the old World. And when they were all settled in, we began all over again, now with the added burden of setting good examples for the newcomers. Novices didn't evolve into Juniors; like nature-manacled caterpillars, we all remained Novices for precisely 750 days, which the inexorable code of the Society of Jesus had ordained should be the gestation period of a butterfly. We all knew that the Novitiate lasted two years—such monumental figures are easy to handle and mean nothing—but sometime in my second year someone came up beside my ear, it may have been another Novice or the Evil Spirit himself, and whispered, "Do you know, there's only a hundred days left?" A hundred days? How long is a hundred days? But ten days later I was murmuring to myself that there were now three months left to go and everyone knew how short a time that was. I had started Counting.

Counting was a not uncommon disease that infected Novices of the second year. It was only rarely fatal, but it was nonetheless an extremely painful affliction. Tradition reported that it had been discovered by one James DiGiorgio, S.J., whose desire to escape the First Probation was so insane that he had calculated down to days, hours and minutes the remaining time to Vow Day and release. He was capable, it was fabled, of rattling off that magic differential in any currency you chose: sheet changes, cornbread mornings or flagellation evenings;

how many rosaries, softball games, genuflections or bowel movements stood between him and Zion. Even now DiGiorgio lounged, filled with calm and remote from the slightest taint of Counting, on the sunny Juniorate side of the refectory, biretta upon his head like a triumphal crown of laurel.

There is even now no comprehending the enormous gulf that separated Novice from Junior in that odd world. It was not simply existential, like the difference between Fathers and Brothers. That we understood and accepted. This was mockingly artificial, based on a calculated privation and bestowal of privilege, all under the roof of the same house. It had not so much to be accepted as gotten through, and, like Zeno's arrow heading toward its impossible target or like a Flying Dutchman adrift in the *Stella Maris* on the Hudson, I suspected I would never arrive. What Zeno's arrow did not have to contend with, however, was the sight of all those flashily feathered ends already adhering to the opposite wall. There in front of me in the dining room before each meal were ranks of Juniors who only yesterday had themselves been Novices. They permitted themselves faint smiles as they faced us during grace, the knowing looks of superior beings who had met Novitiate Regular Order and triumphed over it.

It was the Regular Order's final torture, granting me by its terrible predictability an easy way of calculating exactly how many painful things I had to endure before the pain went away. My day of deliverance was July 31, the Feast of Saint Ignatius of Loyola, the Father of Us All, but more appositely it was exactly two calendar years after I had first knocked on that oaken door. And I could smell it, feel it approaching, see it coming, the morning when the messenger crept into my hovel, shook me awake and said, "There's been some terrible mistake. You are not really a *harijan;* you're a Brahmin and here's your birthright. Sorry, sir." Peripeteia. Deliverance.

The vows that the occasion marked were overwhelmed by the occasion itself. Poverty, chastity and obedience I had embraced from the first moment of the Candidacy. Their formalization now meant no extension of my commitment. Rather, it was the Society of Jesus reaching out to receive me. The Jesuits had tried me in the First Probation, and I had tried myself against their standards. The engagement was over and I was invited to enter into a contract whereby I would accept to live in poverty, chastity and obedience in the Society of Jesus and they accepted to receive me for another thirteen-year probation. Until that other remote day I could still request a release, which was invariably given, and return, with my honorable discharge in the pocket of my rust-colored lounge suit, to the World.

We were supposed to reflect before this solemn step, and so the Novices approaching their vows that July, seven of the nine of us who had come up that driveway two years before—Ray Gorman and Steve Toland had long since returned to the Bronx and Queens—began on July 28 a final three-day retreat. By now the pain was quite perfect. DiGiorgio time, reduced to a crawl by my own obsessive calculations, now all but stopped. I did not need time to reflect; I needed climax. Two years minus three days. And Counting.

At first light on July 31, right on schedule, the Blessed

Seven arose from their tombs and put on not their filthy winding sheets of yore but the raiment of immortality, a new and startlingly black cassock tailored and sewed to the wearer's own body. I picked up the biretta, the peculiarly Jesuit clerical hat that even Saint Ignatius wore in his portraits, carried it casually, almost jauntily in my hand out of the dormitory, out of the ascetory, out of the accursed Novitiate, and descended, as lightly as a liberated butterfly, to the chapel.

The altar was an explosion of flowers, ostensibly for the Feast of Saint Ignatius, but actually for *us*. The lights blazed, and Brother Walzer bestrode his organ and poured it on as we entered the chapel. We had chosen the music ourselves, virtuoso Catholic pap unheard by anyone outside a Jesuit house but filled with sound and schmaltz. And Brother Walzer's overextended *vox humana* contrived to make it sound exactly as maudlin as we had intended. The entire Jesuit community was assembled to witness the moment, while up in the visitors' gallery our parents, relatives and friends beamed happily and sleepily on the glory below.

The vow ceremony occurred in the middle of Mass when each of us would rise in turn from the front pew on the Novices' side of the chapel and approach the sanctuary. The moment was now at hand. I too struggled to my feet, surprised that my knees were consenting to support me. I mounted the steps to the high altar and knelt before the Rector. With bowed head I recited the formula I had surreptitiously begun memorizing a year before: *"Die tricesimo primo, mensis Julii . . . ego voveo paupertatem, castitatem et oboedientiam perpetuam in Societate Jesu . . ."* I rose again, steadier now, turned and went to my place, front row, Juniors' side. The arrow had hit the wall, gone straight in and stood there quivering. *Viva* DiGiorgio! *À bas* Zeno!

The day was a delirium. The extraordinary privilege of talking at breakfast, there amidst my lost and suddenly regained companions of last year. Smiling glances, already tinged with condescension for the wretched Novices on the other side of the dining room. A day of visiting with excited guests, impatient almost that it end so that I could enjoy *being* a Junior, a blissful state that existed *inside* the community and not in the visitors' parlor. I wanted a Jesuit, any Jesuit, to call me "Mister" instead of the suddenly déclassé "Brother."

In the evening there was an immense feast at dinner, and the cathartic din of it shook the refectory walls. I sat there with my biretta posed rakishly on my newly sophisticated brow and loved every single, self-indulgent minute of it. Vow Day was the purest, most perfect pleasure I have ever experienced in my life.

The Juniors lived in quarters that superficially resembled the Novices'. The dormitories with their curtained alcoves were in fact identical. There were ascetories too with the familiar table desks. These were no longer the bare deserts of the ascetic Novice, however, but lush mountain estates covered with verdant blooms bearing the exotic names of *Liddell-Scott's Unabridged Greek Lexicon, Horace: The Complete Odes, Epodes and Satires* and a fat volume from whose ancient spine glowed the golden letters that both promised and delivered my reward *Gradus ad Parnassum,* "Stairway to Heaven," a very secular heaven of Muses and poetry, of richly resonant words and new and dazzling thoughts.

Sometime shortly after vows we began our first class, a course, somewhat inexplicably, in calculus. In my last year in high school I flunked the only course ever in my academic life, trigonometry. I had developed a splendid little block on mathematics, or so I thought. That summer I received an A in calculus, or *the* calculus, as I had very knowingly begun to call it. I had in fact homered on my first at-bat. Two years of Rodríguez had sharpened my eye and perfected my timing. Two years of silence had cleared my head. Two years of scrubbing pots and latrines had put a snap in my arm. The new Junior, a first-round draft pick, was, after two years' seasoning in Triple A, finally ready. I could feel it: I was about to begin on a wild, a stunning, winning streak.

The Novitiate valued observance. The Juniorate, and in fact the rest of the course, expected some recognizable degree of virtue, but as the Master knew very well and as I and others suspected and hoped, it rewarded brains. The pious, it seemed, often had trouble with irregular verbs, with metonymy and synecdoche, with making any sense of Demosthenes, to say nothing of Plato. In a rapidly fading Buffalo sunset the hand of God had suddenly turned to justice. For me, it was just in time.

In the fall, after a triumphal summer of three successive Vow Days, we had all assembled on the lower slopes of Parnassus and settled into what laughingly passed as the Juniorate version of Regular Order. There was no posting of schedules under pale ascetory lights here. Regular Order was still meditation and Mass in the morning and recreation after lunch and dinner. But all the time between, those arid stretches of the Novices' day given over to *manualia* and *mandata,* was diverted entirely and deliciously to going to class and studying. *Laborandum* all but vanished from our vocabulary like some rare Sanskrit phoneme, and on Thursdays and Sundays we unselfconsciously played softball and BASKETBALL or, could one believe it, just sat around and relaxed.

Down the road, on the concrete battleground where men's souls were tried under the guise of basketball, the Juniors were waiting for Chuck, whom they planned to make into a meatball sandwich between Messrs. O'Connell and Navins. Rumor had it that Chuck had spent the last six months of his Novitiate attempting to teach Brother Maguire how to set picks and Brother Neil how to run a give-and-go in some dark corner of the subcloister with a roll of toilet paper as a basketball and a bemused Brother Adel as the only spectator.

It was all for nothing. That first summer the rest of us new boys in town were destined to play mere spectators to the blooding of the Chucker. But he survived, and handsomely. The new Mr. Gilligan, now six feet tall and two hundred pounds of the sheerest determination this side of Aloysius Gonzaga, had also been waiting for them. He had no moves and no speed, but he had bulk, a gunner's eye and a sweetly perfect willingness to kill in the cause of victory.

The first-year Juniors, those of us who survived the Great Basketball War, were called Poets and we read Vergil and Horace, Sophocles and Euripides, Keats and Milton. The second-year were called Rhetoricians and

studied Cicero and Demosthenes and Burke and New-
man. It was a marvelous nineteenth-century English-
university education of the type that Arnold Toynbee
believed he was among the last generation to receive. At
its heart it was untroubled by any science, hard or soft,
and though we read some medieval and early modern
history in our second summer, that was merely a kind of
dessert to match the amusingly imaginative calculus
appetizer. Greek and Latin were the main course, and I
feasted upon them. With all the fervor of a new lover I
memorized Greek lyrics and assigned myself the task of
translating Swinburne's *Atalanta in Calydon* into Greek
verse, the dialogues into Attic iambs, the choruses into
Doric measures of huge complexity.

I passed across a bewildering landscape. We studied the
ancients in English-university editions, and so the Greeks
and the Romans came to us through a late-Victorian haze
where the sensibilities of Jebb and Jowett and Mahaffy
guided our own. It was as if we had been transported in
spirit to the Oxford or Cambridge of seventy-five years
ago, when gentlemen "read Classics" in an atmosphere
immune to the blight of German scholarship or the pricks
of social anxiety. Inside the classroom the sense of lawn
and flannel was almost palpable, but outside were the
sights and sounds and feel not of the Cam or the Isis but
of the Hudson Valley in the first splendor of spring or the
heavy glory of fall.

I had never experienced nature or the seasons before
coming to St. Andrew; they lay somewhere beyond the
urban horizon where I never went. Here the liturgical and
calendar year conspired in close harmony with the en-

vironment to thrust us, indoors and out, into the path of new experiences of the senses. Day after day the Palisades across the Hudson folded into new and unexpected colors. The river was as white and enormous in winter as the chapel was dark and closed in upon itself at 6 A.M. As Easter approached, both liturgy and land thawed, and within a month I could lie out of doors and read Sappho framed upward out of the flowers against a pale-blue sky. Sometimes I catch the lush smell again and suddenly I can see Pindar with his maroon binding and ragged university-press edges lying next to me in the grass.

I have never quite recovered from that extraordinary education. I learned Latin and Greek in a way no undergraduate ever could or did. For all of us, Latin was to some degree a genuinely spoken language. It was not very elegant perhaps, our *cucina latina* as it was called, and not always correct, but it was the classical tongue nonetheless and added an unusual dimension to the study of the texts; Latin became *familiar*. And both Latin and Greek studies were dominated by an elaborate and revealing rhetorical analysis.

I have learned only a few really useful things in my life. One was how to diagram sentences, the almost offhand gift of a nun in grade school, which in high school I discovered could be applied, and even more convincingly, to Latin as well as English sentences. It was a revelation to see the structure of a language exposed to my understanding in such a transparent and comprehensible way. Now in the Juniorate the complementary parts were deftly fitted into place. With Greek, words themselves yielded up their inner constitution, and with rhetorical analysis, paragraphs and entire bodies of composition. I was astonished. I had penetrated a mystery more profound than anything I later discovered in philosophy: I had found out how language and thought worked.

The price was literary. Jesuit education at almost any stage of the course came to an almost audibly grinding halt somewhere just short of the modern experience, not because the latter was thought to be morally threatening but because that's where our textbooks stopped, in that literary twilight zone where the Great Tradition showed disturbing signs of trailing off into some dubious and inscrutable minor key. In the Juniorate our initiation into English poetry ended somewhere in the neighborhood of Tennyson, and though there was a kind of underground attachment to Gerard Manley Hopkins, S.J., there was no real exposure to or understanding of modern poetry. I read some novels in a private, desultory and not very enlightening way, but we never studied the genre. Our English prose fodder was eighteenth-century essayists and nineteenth-century orators. American literature did not seem to exist.

While our contemporaries in the World were at least dabbling in sociology, anthropology and psychology, we and most of the rest of the Society of Jesus ignored the social sciences, which had barely forced themselves into the curricula of Jesuit colleges and not at all into the far more conservative pedagogy that prevailed inside the Jesuits' own houses of study. Our education at this stage was not intended to prepare us for any future work as ministers of the Word or healers of souls but simply to educate us. And that still meant, as it had for so many previous generations, a literary education in the classics, and later in the classics of philosophy. Only far down the long course, when the survivors finally addressed themselves to moral and pastoral theology, would that carefully wrought training program turn its concern toward any souls other than the Jesuits' own.

The emphasis was not entirely unrealistic. Most of us sitting in those sunny classrooms at St. Andrew parsing our way through Plato's *Apology* would spend our Jesuit lives helping students do exactly the same thing in other classrooms. Some might go to the missions or be assigned to give retreats, but in that day the overwhelming number of Jesuits were destined to be educators in Jesuit schools, where their direct pastoral ministrations would be confined to helping out hearing confessions in a neighboring parish on weekends. The Society of Jesus had in fact a few parishes of its own, but it escaped no one's attention that the Fathers assigned there had the heads and hands and batting averages of minor leaguers.

It was not only the moderns we neglected. We lived in ignorance of contemporary literary developments or even events pure and simple. I had had absolutely no contact with the World for four years. Neither the atom bomb nor Norman Mailer had fallen upon me. Art was merely a word, and my only unwitting exposure to its exemplars was in the portraits of the Jesuit founders hung in halls so dark as to be inscrutable and in some Vatican Museum reproductions of Greek and Roman sculpture which showed up in our textbooks; some actually had brown paper pasted over the obligatory Vatican fig leaf, presumably for those easily inflamed by fig leaves. Pablo Picasso was rumored to be a Cuban second baseman who Chuck's athletic grapevine assured him had been traded to the Brooklyn Dodgers.

I regret none of it. On balance, I still prefer to understand rhetoric rather than sociology, and the diagramming of sentences still ranks higher in my pantheon of the practical sciences than rat-running or macroeconomics. I have long since been struck by both the atom bomb and Norman Mailer, but somewhere within there lingers the reserved judgment that Edmund Burke was more explosive than either. Nineteenth-century educations have much to recommend them.

But I had certain extracurricular advantages. At the beginning of my second year I was appointed Juniorate librarian. There was a small library of classical texts and commentaries immediately outside our study hall, but for anything else the Juniors had to make specific request from the catalog of the house library, and I went and fetched it for them. The house library was primarily for the use of the Fathers there, but I too now held its key in my hand. I could read as I pleased, with some splendid hints from my predecessor, who fed voraciously, as I was about to, upon its contents. He suggested I try Evelyn Waugh as a start.

So I did, all of him, and Galsworthy and Dickens. This lofty program was interrupted by the discovery of a gentleman named Krafft-Ebing who began his curious narrative with the tale of a Viennese serving girl who, he noted without trace of moral or aesthetic judgment, was wont to braid her pubic hair. The Preceding was then Confirmed by Example abundant enough to carry me through a week of interested reading. Krafft-Ebing was unmoved, but I, probably because I was unused to the ways of Vienna, thought it was terrific stuff. I composed myself and read on: Huysmans, Van Wyck Brooks and someone I thought was even more terrific than Krafft-Ebing, S. J. Perelman.

As books and study began to reoccupy that place within me which they had deserted two years before, the tension melted away. In part it was merely expectation. The Juniorate I anticipated would be a pleasant, more relaxed place than the Novitiate, and so it was. Part, too, was the regimen. For someone who enjoyed books, languages and intellectual activities, an enjoyment sharpened to desire by two years of absolute drought, the life of classes and study without cares or distractions was a pure delight. But the chief cause of my satisfaction was the capacity to engage, legitimately and even laudably, in something outside myself. The Novitiate held a mirror up to the soul relentlessly illuminated by spiritual self-examination. The Novice was constantly measuring himself against some furtive behavioral ideal that could never be achieved; the Junior returned to the finite, to the simpler, merely human goal of intellectual improvement.

It was in the Juniorate too that we began to grow affectionate toward each other. In the Novitiate we clustered around the Manuductor after lunch and dinner to await our social fate in an assigned band or to try our hobbled tongues on some prepared conversation as we descended and ascended the paths to the Hudson. Or else we faced a Thursday sobered by the thought that even the beloved softball lay on the yonder side of a moral choice.

In the Juniorate recreation was unashamedly recreation. We were turned out of doors to walk or talk with anyone we chose. Moral innuendoes were markedly absent on Juniorate Thursdays, save perhaps in the nice choice of whether to kill or be killed on the basketball court. The less violent walked or played softball—which in the Juniorate degenerated into a mere game, much to Chuck's disgust—or took out their frustrations with Latin indirect discourse by flailing innocuously at trees and bushes in the woods. Whatever you did, it mattered to no one but yourself, not even to God, who we had been led to believe in the Novitiate interested Himself in everything.

The Novitiate smacked of survival, and we all needed allies in that war zone. We touched base with our allies during recreation, that rare commodity which charity constrained us occasionally to squander with someone who was uncongenial or uninteresting or just reserved. When peace broke out in the Juniorate, alliances yielded to friendships. We granted each other some space, and in that more expansive social climate we could explore the company of all those others with whom we had spent two years but who were as unknown as if they had arrived the day before yesterday.

We had, too, a large neutral ground for discussion, our studies, where we were free to like or dislike Homer and Milton without threat to our immortal souls. The clever slowly emerged from hiding. Eamon Brennan kept no civil tongue in his mouth. That splendid organ grew atrophied between his jaws for two solid years for the simple reason that in the Novitiate there was no publicly acceptable laughing matter. There was private laughing matter aplenty, of course, and I could look at Brother Brennan, N.S.J, and inwardly smile because I unerringly knew what he was thinking and it was wicked and malicious and invariably entertaining. Then one bright day in September Mr. Brennan, S.J., the new Junior, stood in the midst of his peers at recreation and offered his unsolicited opinion that William Shakespeare was not only a Catholic but likely a Jesuit as well, and then proceeded to demonstrate in detail both vile and sublime that *Hamlet* was a thinly veiled allegory of certain little-known events in the Danish Province of the Society of Jesus. As the engaging Mr. Brennan warmed to this thesis, tears began to flow from eyes and great waves of laughter lapped against the Palisades across the Hudson. Mr. Suchard, S.J., was seen to snicker, and a certain Mr. Geller, S.J., lapsed into a frenzy and passed a small smile through his constipated lips. It was the end of the Great Ice Age and the beginning of a new era. We were all now fellow conspirators.

The Novitiate was filled with a bewildering variety of devices for self-abnegation, one more ingenious than the next. The Juniorate had equally improbable ways of putting the pieces back together again. When Jesuits sat down to eat, their attention was diverted from the pure bestiality of the act by someone reading to them from a pulpit in the dining room. That task was shared by selected Novices and Juniors in alternating months, but at one dinner each week a Junior took to the rostrum to make essay of delivering a sermon to his captive, pruriently interested and utterly cynical audience of masticating superiors, inferiors and peers. The sermons were intended, one supposed, to give us some pulpit practice for that day in the millennial future when we took our spiritual wares into the World. The results were not encouraging, to put the best face upon it, and under ordinary circumstances those tyro preachers would likely have converted the most pious congregation of Irish nuns back to paganism before the final amen.

On occasion, however, the refectory sermon was the vehicle not for some dubious edification but for the straightforward glorification of the sermonizer. On the eve of the Feast of Saint Peter Canisius, S.J., for example, the best Juniorate student of German delivered a sermon in that language; the long-suffering Blessed Claude de la Colombière, S.J., was doubtfully honored with a French sermon whose grammar was always letter perfect but which was invariably delivered in an accent that would scarcely have passed muster in even a Belgian Juniorate. Saint Robert Bellarmine, S.J., provoked a Latin sermon of considerable elegance from the current Mr. Latinitas. The Novices loved the Latin sermon because they fancied they spoke the language, and they could be observed listening and nodding thoughtfully between swallows.

Kid stuff. Lay Brother stuff. Hors d'oeuvres. The entree was served on the Feast of Saint John Chrysostom in the form of a Greek sermon. It was an impossible tour de force, those thirty-five minutes of glorious and impeccable Attic prose delivered from memory with absolute aplomb to a dumbfounded and uncomprehending audience. It was a heady moment for a twenty-one-year-old, and as I descended the pulpit I understood that now at last I had purged and forgiven all, the Master, the *manualia,* Brother Suchard, even *laborandum.* It was easy to be generous when the mattock in your hand was gold and not iron.

It was not only from the pulpit that life looked new. The Juniors saw, however marginally, the Society of Jesus from within. Perspectives broadened and deepened in some indefinable way, as they would at each successive stage in the course. As Novices we all imagined we would never be able to forget the Novitiate, but we did, and rapidly, even though it continued to pursue its astonishing spiritual business right there under our eyes. And even at this slight distance, it was the Master of Novices rather than the Novices themselves who became the object of some small degree of sympathy, understanding and even admiration. Robert Grissom, it was now clear, had the most difficult assignment in the entire Society of Jesus: he had, by word and relentless example, to make Jesuits; everyone else, Fathers, Brothers and Scholastics, had only themselves to answer for.

My attention began to shift away from the Lay Brothers, who had long since lost their attraction as a rare and exotic species, to the once remote Fathers, many of whom were now our teachers and with whom we had easy but generally very correct relationships. We met on the common ground of the classroom but nowhere else, and though the Juniors now openly and with approval addressed each other on a first-name basis, a familiarity frowned upon in the Novitiate, that practice did not extend beyond the circle of peers: it was still Brother Czajka and Father McCann.

Frank McCann—it is easy now—was the house librarian as well as professor of English for the poetry year, and so I probably spent as much private time with him as any Junior did. I liked and admired him enormously for his intelligence and his cool sophistication, but we never became familiars. There was some easygoing conversation but no unveiling of confidences and, more oddly, little discussion of the intellectual matters that were presumably the chief business between us. Academic instruction, it appeared, ended at the classroom door, and the caste gulf between Father and Scholastic was wider and deeper than the intellectual bond that might have brought together teacher and student.

There may have been another reason as well. It was expressly forbidden for anyone save the Master of Novices to speak to those in their First Probation. That proscription was scrupulously observed, and even the Rector of the house, who was their nominal superior, left the Novices entirely to the care of the Master. But even after the Novitiate, Scholastics were still regarded as undergoing training, and I suspect that most of the Fathers were reluctant to cross over the line between being our teachers, which was their assigned task, and giving anything that remotely resembled advice or counsel, which was the Superior's responsibility.

The Rector of St. Andrew, that demon liturgical speedster John Hudson, S.J., was now our Superior in fact as well as name, but he did not bear the burden alone. As in every Jesuit house, there was there a Father Minister, a kind of executive officer who actually ran the ship, and a Spiritual Father who had the care of our souls. Assignment to these duties seems to have fallen into a pattern in the Jesuits, though of course that least Society savored the occasional extravagant anomaly. Rectors, even those who were not, somehow always contrived to look like Rectors. They enjoyed a kind of distinguished air, like well-polished pewter, possessed excellent table manners, used a soft but distinct diction and cut a nice figure at the high altar during Mass. And if they seemed a trifle worldly at times, it was doubtless by reason of their incessant rubbing up against wealthy Externs whom they were trying to separate from their shiny Catholic money. It seemed like a pleasant and not too difficult occupation, being a Rector.

Though there was no demonstrable connection between being a Novice Manuductor and later becoming a Rector of a Jesuit house, it was perfectly clear that all the Fathers Minister in the entire history of the Jesuits had been Subs in the Novitiate. They had the same hearty and bluff good humor and can-do attitude. They laughed and spoke rather too loudly, lost their tempers and regained them quickly and banged into chapel pews and refectory tables when they walked about the house. Rectors had porcelain hands; Ministers had the savvy hands of Eagle Scouts, which in fact they were. Ministers, you knew, had once played sports, though not very well, and still played cards, rather more successfully. They drank scotch and dreamed of getting out of this assignment and becoming a chaplain in the Armed Forces.

All Spiritual Fathers had once given retreats to earn their keep, and before that they had taught Latin and religion in a Jesuit high school. But that was a long time ago. Now they were merely old and gray, gentle souls resting before retirement, reading the *Times* in the morning and drinking port in the Fathers' recreation room after dinner. They preached an exceedingly mild form of spirituality to their charges on the rare occasions when their counsel was sought out. Otherwise they heard the confessions of the Jesuit community to which they were assigned, and that seemed just fine to everyone concerned. Spiritual Fathers were the objects of effusive but skin-deep affection during the Juniorate and Philosophy and were thereafter ignored except on their jubilees.

John Hughes, S.J., fulfilled his responsibilities toward the Juniors by giving an occasional conference, but they were mere faint carbons of the Master's attention-getting colloquies. They possessed a vague spiritual air but seemed to be about nothing in particular, and we regarded them exactly as such. The Rector as a matter of fact intervened only very slightly in our lives, and his deputy in our midst, the Juniorate Beadle, was an equally ghostly negative of his Manuductor counterpart. He sat at his desk in the rear of the Juniors' ascetory awaiting from the Rector messages that never came.

To all appearances we were on our own. There was little individual guidance of any sort, either then or later, but we were still a community and moved in the community rhythms of eating, sleeping, praying, recreating and going to class. But we now took our own spiritual temperature and shared it with no one. The initiative was now individual, and the vastness of that new situation vis-à-vis the Master's earlier role in my life seemed more like a release than a promotion to a new responsibility.

Our progress was not going unobserved, however, in somewhat more remote quarters of the Society of Jesus. The Novitiate universe revolved so remarkably around the Master of Novices that we were generally unaware that each of us belonged as well to another, greater system—the New York Province and the Society of Jesus as a whole. We were too minuscule particles to make any impression on that latter world as yet, but when we passed out of the Master's orbit we entered in some perceptible way into the workings of the provincial system and its still-mysterious agents who would steer our future course through the Jesuits. Somewhere on the campus of Fordham University sat the Father Provincial, the Superior of the fifteen hundred Jesuits who composed the New York Province. The United States was then divided into eight such provinces: California, Chicago, Maryland, Missouri, New England, New Orleans, Oregon and New York, which was numerically the largest, even though it embraced only New York City, Jersey City and Buffalo.

With the end of the Juniorate we would receive our first real assignments. We would all go on to the next stage of the course, Philosophy, and most to the Jesuit house of studies at Woodstock, Maryland, where the Scholastics of the New York and Maryland Provinces worked over Aristotle and Saint Thomas under the same roof. But not all. Some at least might be sent elsewhere, and that decision rested with someone in the Provincial's office at Fordham, on the advice of someone at St. Andrew. We were being reported upon, though no one knew how or by whom, and material on each of us was accumulating, and would continue to accumulate, in Province dossiers in New York and eventually in Rome as well, where the Father General observed and ruled his thirty-two thousand troops all over the world, from New York, the largest of all, to the twenty-two Jesuits of the Rumanian Vice-Province and the eight mysterious figures who toiled *Ad Majorem Dei Gloriam* in remote Lithuania-Estonia.

Something was stirring in my head. The World, which knew better about such things, would probably call it ambition, but that was not an acknowledged virtue of the religious life and so what was registering was not that taboo notion but something more soothingly described as the widening of horizons, the recognition of possibilities. Our futures were gliding almost imperceptibly toward our hands, and I reached out and attempted to take hold of mine. I suggested—I did not yet request; even that was too bold—that I might be sent not to Woodstock but rather to St. Louis University, where the Scholastics of the Missouri Province studied philosophy and where I could also do additional work in Latin and Greek.

It was the blindest of blind shots. Every year a few Scholastics were sent into other provinces to pursue philosophy and even overseas when it came time to do theology. Who was sent where and why was never entirely clear in a world where all orders were stamped "Perfect Obedience"; why a Philosopher might be sent to Missouri or Chicago or New England, for example, but never to New Orleans or California or Oregon. Several were dispatched annually from New York to St. Louis—the Missouri Province never reciprocated, perhaps because the Eastern moral climate at Woodstock was deemed too debilitating for Midwestern Jesuits—most willy-nilly for reasons known only to the Provincial, but a few to study something quite specific at the university. In my rapidly opening eyes the university looked like a plum. I asked for it and I got it.

My first four years as a Jesuit were over. In that time I had been visited by parents and relatives six or seven times and by other vagrant, unannounced but welcome friends on two or three other occasions. I had slept under no other roof except for the two exotic weeks at Auriesville. I had not seen a newspaper or listened to a radio or seen a movie in all that time. Four years of the life of the World had fallen out of my life, with no great consequence, I imagine. We were informed and entertained in other ways and on other matters; we had adapted to another culture as remote and exotic from that of our contemporaries as that of an Ainu or a Trobriand Islander. I was stuffed full of meditation, cornbread, softball and Sophocles. I was girt with cincture and chain. I had survived both Brother Geller and Brother Gilligan and a twice-daily examination of conscience besides. I was pronounced ready to move on to the next stage of what was nicely described as my "formation."

VIII

The Perennial Philosopher

In June I was told that I was being sent, together with
Messrs. Houghton and McGarry, to study philosophy at
St. Louis University. In that day, flight was judged far too
heady stuff for mere Scholastics, and so we were dispatched into the Midwestern void on what was then the
Pennsylvania Railroad. The journey took twenty-one
hours and seventeen minutes.

It should have been exciting, that voyage into the Great
World after four years of domestic internment at St.
Andrew on Hudson. It was not. The train was hot, dirty
and slow, and though the company was certainly familiar—we had spent every waking hour of the past four
years in each other's company—it was not greatly entertaining. McGarry was the strong, silent, solid type, and
Tony Houghton, who was even more solid, was an
honors graduate of the Christopher Looney School of
Liturgical Conversation. More, he may have been the

only human being ever to flog himself in an upper berth outside Altoona, Pennsylvania.

I watched out the dirty windows as America became flat and spacious and unexpectedly empty. St. Andrew was, it seemed to me, a fragment of the city inexplicably set down in the midst of a park a few hours out of New York, and so I suppose I expected people lined up cheek by jowl all across the country. But nobody was out there, and it finally began to dawn upon me that I was leaving here for an unknown and unfamiliar there. We crossed a broad, dull river that bore no resemblance to the Mississippi of my imaginings and passed into a faceless city that meant only one thing to me: a National League baseball team resided in St. Louis. It was not a premise to build a life upon.

But there was a kindness there, too. At Union Station our fellow expatriates from New York awaited us. McNaughton had already been there two years; Scally and Meagher had arrived the year before from St. Andrew. I was reassured by the familiarity of the faces, the voices, the picking up of well-worn themes. And they were pleased to see us: for Jesuits every novelty, a new face, a chance visitor, a change of assignments, was as momentous as a change to the gold standard or a lunar calendar. They smiled upon us and whispered their first ominous little joke. Was it true I had *asked* to come there?

We got off to what seemed like a rather odd start. Our veteran hosts did not take us directly from Union Station to the Jesuit house. We went instead to the immense Anheuser-Busch brewery, where we presented ourselves, in some fierce parody of what had occurred at St. Andrew four years earlier, at the oaken front door and requested the visitors' tour of the works. We got it, with a vengeance, and after we had paid our respects to the Clydesdales we sat down in a kind of *bierstube* and drank free Budweiser for the rest of the afternoon.

This was, as it turned out, a not uncommon Saturday occupation for some of the New York Scholastics. By the end of three years I would have taken that tour often enough to have memorized it—"Yes, the main brewery covers an area as large as the Loop in Chicago"—all to reach the magic *bierstube* where the "young Fathers" were permitted to sit on after the other visitors had left and drink to their clerical hearts' content. I knew that if I ever left the Jesuits, I could always get a job as a brewery guide. Or as a Clydesdales' groom.

The Jesuit university was a large urban institution in the middle of St. Louis. Its chief buildings filled an entire city block and were arranged around a concrete courtyard. On one side of the quadrangle was the Philosophate, the residence of the Jesuit Scholastics engaged in this new stage of their course of studies. Some of our professors lived with us in the same building, but most of the Jesuit faculty of the university lived in a cloistered section of the main university building next door, where the chapel and the community dining hall were also located. The hundred-odd Scholastics in residence there took their recreation in the concrete quad, had their classes in the Philosophate and had little or no contact with the other students and faculty of the university, even though we were living there in the midst of them.

The Scholasticate at St. Louis was unusual for its day.

OURS

Originally, Jesuit houses of study were set down in the midst of the great cities of Europe and little thought was given to segregating even Novices from the World that swirled around them. But at some point, likely in the mischievous nineteenth century, the original concept was replaced by the strikingly inane notion that men preparing for the spiritual conquest of the World would best be trained in the woods.

Jesuits in the United States fell to buying every acre of bog, bayou and wilderness they could find, and in spite of Socrates' clear warning that he had never learned anything from a tree, the Scholastics were shipped en masse to those leafy bowers and bosky glades engagingly named Florissant, Woodstock, French Lick, Shrub Oak and Spring Hill. There among the lowing kine the future intellectuals of the Church spent fifteen years girding themselves for combat. It was a near-perfect preparation for becoming a veterinarian or a tree surgeon.

No tree surgeons we. We were going to live and study in the city, as the encounter with Mr. Busch's maltworks already so brilliantly suggested. And for the first time in our Jesuit lives, each in his own room. The one assigned to me excited considerable interest. It was, admittedly, a rather queer place, a very long and narrow room that rejoiced in the name of the "Bowling Alley." But that was not the point of the admiration, as I immediately discovered. No sooner was I shown my room than Scally, Meagher and McNaughton were in it at my heels. The door was locked and the transom opened. Cigarettes were produced. My God, we could smoke!

Well, not exactly. They *did* smoke, but since it was

done without permission, it not only had to be done very, very privately; the smoke had also to be undetectable in the hall outside, and that depended on the prevailing winds. In some rooms the breezes seemed always to be billowing in the window and so out the transom and into the hall. The Bowling Alley, on the other hand, was one of those golden domiciles where the draft almost always came in the transom and went wafting, with great billows of cigarette smoke in its wake, *out* the window. As it turned out, I had been assigned the meteorologically perfect room for smoking.

It took me five minutes in that company to regain a smoking habit now four years disused. And once acquired, it consumed, for me and for the others, an inordinate amount of time and energy. Smoking became not just a mindless act but an occupation. We were always on the lookout for a time and a place. It disrupted study and it disrupted recreation. It disrupted our lives.

Since I now possessed the Bowling Alley, I became host to smokers at all hours of the day and night. Protocol demanded that the smoker provide his own cigarettes and ashtray, a metal typewriter ribbon case, and I generously supply the sanctuary. The smokers generally protected their privacy with a universal Jesuit "Do Not Disturb" signal, a handkerchief knotted around the outside doorknob of a room. It usually meant that the occupant was deeply engrossed or, more likely, taking a nap, gracefully called a "siesta" by the Jesuits, and to give credibility to this the smoker usually drew the window shade to cast what might appear from the outside as a sleepy pall upon the room. A casual visitor might have thought that the

Missouri Philosophers spent most of their time sleeping.

We did spend a lot of time in the sack. At St. Andrew a nap was almost totally unknown, as well it might be in a dormitory. But here we had our own rooms—and a 5 A.M. rising hour. The siesta was probably another Jesuit importation from Rome or Spain, like the quaint injunction in the Rules that the windows should be kept closed at night, presumably against the nocturnal miasma so beloved of Europeans, but whatever its origins, the siesta was a ferocious waste of time in a community of twenty-two-year-olds. We got up too early in the morning and so dozed through meditation; we slept too long in the afternoon and so went to bed too late at night.

There were other ways of wasting time as well. After four totally unalcoholic years, we were now served beer at dinner, huge pitchers of it, probably provided at a clerical discount by our friends at Anheuser-Busch. It was generally consumed in moderation, but on certain evenings, by some common and mysteriously attested assent, a few of us dove headlong into the dinner tankards, and then, instead of going to the common recreation in the dark quadrangle outside, we mounted uncertainly through the dim stairways to the turreted and gabled roof of the main university building. There we sat and smoked into the evening, gazing down on the lights of the Queen City of the Mississippi and cursing the fate that had brought us to that pesthole. It was a miracle that no one fell off.

That pesthole was largely of our own making. The New York and Maryland Scholastics clung closely together at St. Louis as a form of mutual protection against what we discerned as Midwestern barbarism. Those bland

and feckless farm boys from Milwaukee and Omaha with their gold-filled teeth and odd accents were the objects of our deep and relentless disdain, a scorn passed from generation to generation of new arrivals from the East. In the course of three years our disdain mellowed somewhat as we discovered our common Jesuit humanity, but it never entirely disappeared because we never permitted it to.

We became outlanders in our homeland as well. Each Province published an annual catalog listing the location, house by house, of its every Jesuit member and describing, in an arcanely abbreviated Latin, his assignment. By migrating to St. Louis in the Missouri Province we were cast into a special limbo at the end of the catalog reserved for those *Degentes extra Provinciam,* "Living Outside the Province." My new function was plainly and humbly described there among the St. Louis *Auditores Philosophiae, anno primo.*

There were far more interesting and exotic things in that book, however. Out on remote Truk, Pater Georgius Flattery was by now *Sup. resid., quasi-paroch., Min., Mod. foed. SS. Cord. et Sod. B.V.M. Truk, exam. cand.,* the last of which meant that should some confused Trukese present himself as a candidate for the Novitiate, P. Flattery would examine him on his softball and grammatical skills, provided, of course, that George's other strenuous duties as Superior, Moderator of the Confraternity of the Sacred Heart and of the Sodality of the Blessed Virgin (Truk) permitted. The Reverend Flattery had two Jesuit subjects in his community, one a Father whose duty it was to "conduct missions in the northern and western isles" (the vagueness of their name and location suggested that the anonymous Latin scribe of the catalog had as little idea of the geography of the Caroline Archipelago as the rest of us) and a Brother Whelan whose assignment was simply *Ad omn.,* "everything else."

Some entries in the catalog were mysterious, others frightening. At the "College of St. Ignatius" in Manhasset—I can bear personal witness that there was nothing remotely resembling a college there—dwelled the interesting Walter Tortuga, who, like some creature out of Kafka, was eternally *Exspect. destin.,* "awaiting his assignment," while here and there in the pages of the catalog were salted away forty- or fifty-year-old Scholastics whose assignments were described, almost touchingly, as simply *Orat pro Soc.,* "He is praying for the Society," to which was occasionally added, in an ominous parenthesis, "(Outside the House)."

Who those unfortunates were and what went wrong to terminate their training in midcourse, no one knew except possibly their exact contemporaries. Whoever they were, the Society of Jesus had accepted responsibility for them when they took their vows, and Jesuits they remained, eternal Scholastics who had stumbled over some physical or psychic misfortune and would go no further toward the priesthood. They lived out their lives in quiet obscurity in some Jesuit mission or else "outside the house" in a mental institution, each with the single but sufficient Jesuit task of "praying for the Society."

We who were young and sound and reasonably sane were amused by these curious and often impenetrable

Latin descriptions of how Ours spent their time. On the wall of my Bowling Alley hung a large framed photo of a derelict sitting disconsolately on his filthy cot in some flophouse. It now bore a new title: *Degens extra Provinciam,* "Outside the Province," and underneath, in smaller letters, *Fumat pro Soc.,* "He is Smoking for the Society."

In September our courses began: logic, epistemology, cosmology, the history of philosophy. From the outset it was clear that the object was not to philosophize but to study philosophy, or, more specifically, the Aristotelian-Thomistic synthesis that then reigned supreme in Jesuit and, in fact, all Catholic seminaries and throughout the Church. And we studied it in a peculiarly hybrid manner that cross-bred the scholastic method of the thirteenth century with the new mechanics of the age of the textbook.

We were presented a list of seventy propositions in Latin drawn from the core courses of our curriculum: epistemology, cosmology, metaphysics, ethics, psychology and natural theology. These were all "rational sciences"—that is, they were developed by the human intellect working independently of revelation, though revelation stood close at hand, of course, to guide our intellects and occasionally whisper hints about the correct answers. At the end of two years each of us would be expected to seat himself in front of a board of four or five faculty examiners and rehearse, in form, the "defense" of any of these seventy theses they might choose.

"*Bene,* Mister, *velim demonstres thesim sextam sub theologia naturali.*"

Thesis Six? A piece of *crustella.*

"Thesis sic ponitur: Deus solus est aeternus, immensus et omnipraesens."

There followed the graceful gavotte first devised at the University of Paris more than half a millennium earlier. *"Definitio . . . status quaestionis . . . syllogistice sumptum . . . proinde ad minorem . . . distinguo . . . ut Epicurus et sequaces ejus et quidam moderni aiunt . . . Atqui contra . . . Cadit, immo vero ruit thesis adversariorum . . . quod erat demonstrandum!"*

For two years we sat in classrooms three or four hours a day preparing for that moment of *veritas* when we would gracefully pirouette to the defense of theses that no one of us was inclined to doubt, much less deny. To teach us the steps, the same theses were laid out in detail in Latin textbooks prepared by Jesuit authors at the twin citadels of authentic Thomism, the Pontifical Institutes at Rome and Toronto. No fair memorizing, of course. We had to be ready to deal with a bewildering variety of curves, change-ups and sliders thrown up at us like wily old southpaws by our professors. We were supposed to think fast and accurately and *in form.* A terrible legacy! I still have problems with people who don't think *in form,* which is to say, with almost everyone on the face of the planet.

Most of the theses could be found in Thomas Aquinas, though not so neatly as they were framed for us, and, if one looked very carefully, in Aristotle as well, though he sometimes got the answers wrong. So we wandered back and forth between our textbooks and Thomas' *Summa Theologia,* with an occasional foray into the *Metaphysics* for the brave, while the eye and the head and the tongue grew sharp with disputation.

Philosophy was occasionally fun but nowhere as engaging for me as my encounter with the Classics at St. Andrew. I enjoyed the verbal acrobatics, the multiple and subtle distinctions and the finely crafted products that emerged from our scholastic workbenches, but I was not much interested in the subject, which seemed to me to have far less to do with reality than what Sophocles and Demosthenes had to say and was surely far less elegant in the saying.

It was not fun for everyone. There were some exceedingly bright people in those classes and some few who even then were showing signs of sinking beneath the waves. And drowning? I do not know. I was never privy to anyone's reasons for leaving the Jesuits or indeed whether anyone was asked to leave on academic or any other grounds. We were all screened before entry, and somewhere in that process a judgment must have been made on the likelihood that this candidate could handle the course of studies and that other could not. What was obvious was that now, four or five years into the academic program, some were very good students at everything they put their hand to, and some others had very special aptitudes for this discipline or that, while a number were struggling every day with every page of every text they were set to read.

I'm inclined to think that very few of these latter were ever told to depart, that they were in effect too dim to have a vocation. Something else occurred. In Theology a dual track appeared, one branch called the "Long Course," the other, somewhat less complex path of study the "Short Course." The Long Course led directly to full profession, the four vows, absolute Jesuithood, so to speak. The Short Course also led to ordination to the priesthood but to a somewhat lesser form of profession— the Vow of Obedience to the Pope was omitted. The Short Course was for the strugglers, the intellectually mediocre, the not-exactly-brightest-and-best. The Professed Fathers of Four Vows were the true Jesuit elite: only they could hold the highest offices in the Society of Jesus. Everyone pretended that it was a distinction without a difference; everyone also knew exactly who had come through the Long Course and who had not.

That distinction did not yet exist in fact at St. Louis, but the candidates for one track or the other were already discernible as we were put through our paces in the classroom. And yet we were all being terribly wasted, we young student Scholastics, and in a familiar way. Regis High School had skimmed the cream off New York parochial schools and turned some of them into bright and nimble wits who could perform a variety of intellectual operations but who had little or no sense of the intellectual life or its values. We frequently put our mouths where our heads should have been. Nor is it difficult to see why: our Jesuit teachers had been trained in an almost identical fashion. Now at age twenty-five we should have been coming into our own. Instead, we were sitting in lecture courses where the only discussion had to do with the mechanics of demonstration.

The problem was that we were studying blueprints and

not philosophy. The Philosophate was our intellectual Novitiate. The Juniorate was simply an education, a trifle old-fashioned perhaps, but liberal and humane in the great tradition. And no one, I suspect, has ever suffered great harm from reading Homer or Euripides. But there was a different agenda in the Philosophate. We were having laid down for us the conceptual foundations upon which the great edifice of Catholic dogma was reared. We were not taught that dogma as such—that would come later in Theology—but its shadow was upon us and we were certainly not "reading philosophy" in the same humanistic fashion in which we had "read Classics" in the previous two years. The theses, which seemed to flow so effortlessly from human reason, were in fact "potted." If they were dislodged or questioned or threatened, it is conceivable that the dogma, official and unofficial, that rested upon them might also be shaken, and that was purely and simply unacceptable.

We rarely discussed philosophy outside of class, never argued about the highly arguable matter that was being put before us. I neither believed nor disbelieved what I was being taught; it seemed to be logical and it made sense and so I left it at that. And the *adversarii* of each thesis, those pagans, heretics, apostates and Dominicans buried in the footnotes who took an unfortunately differing view of God, man and the universe, were refuted so succinctly and yet so devastatingly that I imagined them very wrongheaded indeed. What, after all, did Descartes and Kant really know about the *philosophia perennis?*

In the third year of philosophy we turned our attention to "special questions," those philosophical conundra which could not be squeezed very comfortably into our seventy theses. The special questions I found no more interesting than the earlier ordinary ones, though they did more directly reveal Thomas' and Aristotle's own more complex view of things. And the third year also gave me an opportunity of pursuing more graduate courses in Greek at the university.

The Classics Department at St. Louis University was small, and though most of the students enrolled in it were Scholastics, the faculty were all laymen. It was easy work and it must have been an equally pleasant task for our professors to teach graduate students who had been so thoroughly immersed in Greek and Latin that they could sight-read the first and speak the second. We read the texts the way graduate students did, not in the sunny Oxford style of the Juniorate but in the cloudier and more somber mode of Tübingen. A rather solemn but good-natured gentleman named Korfmacher introduced me to Aristophanes. Four of us sat before him and pondered text and *apparatus criticus* while Professor Korfmacher pondered his sear and yellow notes and carefully explained to us from them all the botanical *hapax legomena* in what I had previously thought were comedies. But the texts were at least unexpurgated and at last I could look at the fig leaves in the illustrations in all their suggestive integrity.

The Scholasticate at St. Louis generated a peculiar sense of confinement. At St. Andrew we had an immense estate to wander over, which we often did by command or by choice. Here we now were in the midst of a large city, and neither I nor the others much ventured to explore it. Museums, galleries and libraries were all there for our visiting, but I got no closer to them than my bleary nighttime perch atop the gabled roof. At the end of three years I had as little sense of St. Louis or the people who lived there as I had on the day I arrived, except that now I could find my own way to the brewery.

Afternoons and evenings we strolled the quad, but on Thursdays, still our day off, there was a special treat on the order of a trip to Esopus. The Scholastics were bussed out to a bare and almost unfurnished house on the banks of the Missouri to make our holiday revels. The revels were chiefly lunch, walking through the fields of the Jesuit property or staring at the disconsolate Missouri. I had already stared for long hours at the disconsolate Mohawk and this was not very much better or different. We were also given brief looks at the World. We had the daily papers and *Time* magazine in our recreation room, were permitted to listen to the news on the radio and were occasionally shown a carefully chosen movie in which Van Johnson and Keenan Wynn always seemed to make an appearance. If you wanted to see a *real* movie, you had to follow another route, the one that led invariably to Gary Breen.

Mr. Gary Breen, S.J., arrived in St. Louis the same time I did. He had grown up in New Jersey but latterly made a bad move to Washington, D.C., and Gonzaga High School, which put him firmly in the bosom of the Maryland Province. In the tradition of that Province, Gary Breen was not a towering intellectual—*Mens nulla in corpore sano* was the libelous New York version of the motto of the Maryland Province—but he had a very advanced case of the Jesuit smarts.

Not long after his arrival in St. Louis, Gary was running some kind of scam that won him the unofficial title of "Brother Buyer." He was our dealer. He had apparently unlimited access to cigarettes and could get you booze if you really craved that. Need three rolls of Super X film? Brother Buyer could get it for you. Slides or prints? He had pals among the Lay Brothers, and he must have had some cash, possibly from his parents. Nobody knew for sure; nobody much cared. And Brother Buyer was both generous and discreet.

Gary Breen and I became fast friends. He had far more nerve than I, which I admired. I talked a great game, but he played it. He discovered the university gym and talked us into varsity basketball practices. In return I cut him in on a closely guarded New York secret. There was a Regis alumnus living in St. Louis. No one remembered who discovered him six or seven years previously, but his friendship was passed down from year to year among the New York Scholastics like a precious Kabbalistic talisman. What Ray Brunschweiger actually possessed was not the *Clavis Sapientiae* but a television set, and on frequent Saturday afternoons during football season we put on our black suits and clerical collars and ambled over to the Brunschweiger living room, where we drank beer and watched Notre Dame take on the godless hordes of Michigan State on the tube.

Brother Buyer was dealt into this private New York racket because we all owed him. On one notable occasion he produced two tickets to a Cardinal game at Sportsman's Park. He and I went off on Saturday afternoon in high exhilaration at the coup, but unfortunately we were observed, probably by some uncompassionate Father who either knew that Scholastics were not supposed to be at baseball games or else was annoyed that Brother Buyer had gotten better seats. Gary Breen always went first class. We were reported at any rate, and were instructed to take a *culpa* at dinner.

The *culpa* was an old friend from Novitiate days. With the permission of the Superior you could make a public manifestation of your faults before the community at dinner. You said grace out in the middle of the refectory, and then after grace, but before the reading began, you knelt there in full view of all and with arms outstretched proclaimed *alta voce:* "Reverend Fathers and Dearly Beloved Brothers in Christ, I accuse myself of . . ."

These were generally volunteer performances, and the faults were innocuous enough to cause little distraction from the passage of the beer pitchers around the dining tables. But when Brother Buyer and I knelt out there that evening awaiting the end of grace, the entire Philosophate knew that this was no volunteer mission. We had been nailed, but for what? In this particular art form, style was all, and Gary, once our sentence had been assigned, was, as always, direct: "All right, you have the mouth. What do we say tonight?"

Grace was ended and the silence was now total. The beer sat unmoving on the tables. "Reverend Fathers and Dearly Beloved Brothers in Christ, I accuse myself of recreating outside the assigned times." The Superior's soup spoon paused between bowl and lips and froze there as Brother Buyer repeated the same doubtless heartfelt but distinctly unenlightening self-accusation. We rose and took our places at table. A number of birettas were imperceptibly tipped in our direction, signaling that kind of ultimate admiration reserved for those close scrapes with mortal danger that leave the lion tamer, the escape artist, the high-wire aerialist shaken but brilliantly intact. What in hell had we done?

We were not always so fortunate or so clever. Gary and I smoked away many evenings atop the gabled roofs and altogether too many in the Bowling Alley, which had begun to smell like an opium crib in Tangier. At the beginning of our second year we were all assigned new rooms, as was usual. Brother Buyer and I now found ourselves in rooms next to and across from Father Buchhasser, the tiny Prussian martinet who was the Minister for the Scholasticate, in an area knowingly and derisively called "The Infield," where suspected miscreants were kept under surveillance. Only a fool would smoke in "The Infield," so we went to Jack Flynn's room.

Jack Flynn had just arrived in St. Louis from St. Andrew and he did not as yet smoke. But he lived in one of those meteorological paradises on the fourth floor, and so while Jack went to recreation Gary and I often repaired to his room and smoked. One afternoon we were sitting there smoking, even though the billows of nicotine hung inconclusively and dangerously over the transom. Suddenly there was an authoritative knock on the door. We exchanged paralyzed glances that said "Don't move." Whatever it was did not go away. Gary's lips formed

"Did you lock the door?" I shrugged in horror. The knob turned. It *was* locked. A voice, a Buchhasser voice: "I know you're in there." This was serious. Footsteps went across the hall and dragged back a chair. The unprincipled bastard was going to look through the transom! Now we moved, silently and swiftly, and flattened ourselves against the wall just next to the door. Buchhasser peered through the transom and saw only smoke; Brother Buyer and I had miraculously reduced ourselves more than the proverbial cubit by prayer alone. The doorknob turned again furiously, and then baffled steps retreated down the hall. After five indescribable minutes, we bolted.

Philosophate legend had it that Gary Breen stayed in bed for three days and three nights with the covers pulled over his head and a knotted handkerchief on his door-knob. I tried to be more casual, but the results were identical: there were notes in our mailboxes bidding us see the Superior. It could have been worse. He didn't accuse us directly of being Buchhasser's tormentors, but he did confront us with the generic fact of our smoking. We weren't supposed to be smoking, it was that simple, and we were. I promised I would stop. I didn't, but a more drastic solution was taking shape in my head.

I needed a rest and I got one. Along with siesta, American Jesuits had inherited the custom of "villa." Together with the rest of the population, the early Jesuits cleared out of Rome in August and headed for the hills, where they had a summer villa. So every summer the Jesuit Scholastics were sent off to "villa," some more friendly climate where they could relax without depriving themselves of that most treasured of all commodities, each other's company. No Father was ever seen at "villa." They simply and succinctly left town.

The summer camping grounds of the Missouri Province Scholastics was a place inevitably called Loyola Villa and located near Waupaca in the lake country of central Wisconsin. It was lovely. We lived in a wooden frame house on the edge of one of the lakes that stretched endlessly in chains away from us. We made our annual eight-day retreat there, and then for the next seven weeks we played softball, swam, sailed the lakes and ate ourselves into a soft oblivion.

Once a week a truck roared up to our back door, a native of the region threw out a pile of bound newspapers and shouted, "Here they are, boys." What "they" were could have been either the *Waupaca Times,* which he was delivering, or its almost unique contents, pictures of fetching young ladies in bathing suits who were spending the summer on the lakes.

Those glorious maidens must have been out there somewhere—"Miss Arlene Schneider of Chicago, summering at the Crystal Lake bungalow of Mr. and Mrs. Roger Lucey in Appleton"—unless they were a complete hoax fabricated to enliven our summers, but we never saw them, though we wore out the sea lanes of Crystal Lake. We had come a long way from the *Stella Maris.* Here we traveled by canoe, usually for picnics and usually in groups of six or so. We chose our own companions—nobody much worried about "mixing" anymore—made our lunch, loaded it and ourselves into the canoes and made off in search of the phantom bathing beauties. They had the good sense to stay well clear of us, and so we usually ended up eating and playing cards in some remote and beautiful grove.

Those were our two summer anodynes, eating and playing bridge. We never played cards at St. Andrew, but in other Jesuit venues it must have been a more common pastime, since there were a number of already accomplished bridge players at St. Louis. Some played steadily and with an almost Gilliganian intensity right through the summer villa, all day and much of the night, and there was a bridge game on most of our picnics.

Bridge, like philosophy, did not much engage my interest, and I made a poor partner for Brother Buyer's more polished, practiced and entirely ruthless style of play. I was easily distracted from the card count, and as we sprawled out under the trees to take on Kevin Quinlan and Jerry Travis, Brother gave a minatory riff of the cards to collect my wandering internal senses. It was no use. Even as the cards were being dealt I was wondering how long it would be before Travis started splattering his hand all over the blanket and shouting, "This is a lay-down" at the rest of us. Travis had little tolerance for playing out hands he had already won in his own fevered and unmathematical head.

We had been caught in a downpour on our way out to this picnic spot and we were all still damp and dripping when we sat down to play. Quinlan was a large young man, and like large young men he usually preferred to keep his T-shirt on with his swimming trunks. Today, however, he had removed his shirt to dry, and as he dealt the cards his obese chest shook with the suggestion of breasts. And something more. "One diamond." "One heart." I stared. There was no mistaking it. On his left breast were the scars where the large letters "JESUS" had been carved into his chest.

"Three hearts." At twenty-four Kevin Quinlan was already one of the class acts of the Missouri Province. He was undoubtedly intelligent—he could not only play philosophy, as most of the bright and verbal could; he also appeared to understand it—and more: all his personal lines were open to pious Missourians, remote Chicagoans, partying Marylanders and other assorted Magi from the East. He may have played right field in Novitiate softball games, but Kevin Quinlan would one day be pitching for the Missouri Province, no mistake.

"Six spades." Quinlan had some kind of serious streak in his makeup, but he hardly seemed like a fanatic. I tried to imagine the circumstances when he had carved "JESUS" onto his left breast—I dismissed, too quickly perhaps, the possibility that someone else had done it for him or to him. A burst of extravagant adolescent piety in high school, a hot breath from the mouth of the Holy Spirit which blew him right into the Jesuits? A moment of splendid ecstasy in the depressing trough of the Long Retreat? Some coldly brooded contract with God knows what terms and witnessed only by the Master of Novices and the Ministering Angels?

What madness had we here? "Seven no trump." After five Jesuit years I thought I had everyone pretty well figured, even with the dearth of internal or confessional evidence. But in the swift blinking of an eye I knew I had Kevin Quinlan nowhere near figured. Was I the only one in this world who was what he appeared to be? Was Jack Scally into dark and mysterious rites I could not even suspect? Was Gary Breen . . . I looked up to see Brother Buyer's predatory eye staring in total disbelief at the dummy hand I was brightly spreading before him on the blanket. He carefully lit a cigarette with his Dunhill lighter before he trusted himself to speech. "My dear Brother in Christ. Why don't you take a very long walk while I tear this troublesome little seven no trump you signaled out of the amateur hands of Mr. Quinlan and Mr. Travis? Your lead, I think, Mr. Travis."

Brother was usually better company, and on picnics he surpassed his own near-legendary feats of procurement. He produced camera and film, unspeakable edibles not even dimly imagined on the house menu, unopened decks of cards, a portable radio and binoculars. Since most of this was highly contraband, and to avoid giving scandal to the innocent (to say nothing of other, graver consequences), we contrived to carry much of it in the athletic supporters of our bathing suits, which would nicely account for both the excited cries of the newspaperman and the prolonged absence of the legendary nubiles.

The first villa at Waupaca was relaxing and entertaining, but eight weeks is a long time to spend in anyone's woods, and I could already foresee a diminishing enthusiasm for this Jesuit institution. The following summer at Loyola Villa confirmed my suspicion. The novelty was gone and I was long past the day when I could chuck books and studies and simply rusticate. It had a certain historical interest, however. Though I was unaware of it at the time, one afternoon, there under the trees in Wisconsin, I was playing the last softball game of my Jesuit life. I went 0 for 3.

Given a fat pitch, I could still hit the long ball on

occasion. By my third year in St. Louis what had once been an atrocious New York City accent was sufficiently intelligible to permit my being appointed one of the refectory readers. Refectory reading was intended as a form of edification during meals. It was equally often a combat, a peculiarly Jesuit form of combat between the Scholastic reader and the Prefect of Reading, the Father whose assigned task it was to catch mispronunciations. When he did, he pressed a button next to his plate that lit a small red light on the reading stand in the pulpit. The reader paused, penitent, and either corrected himself, with a small tip of his biretta to express his thanks at having this pecadillo revealed, or else waited for the Father to bawl out, over the clatter of knives and forks, "No, Mister; that's hercúlean." Which came as news to me. The reader was supposed to prepare beforehand, to look up the pronunciation of dubious words. We winged it a lot, but who ever heard of "hercúlean"? He was right, of course. He was always right.

I was reading one evening from typical refectory fare, *A History of the Jesuits in the Middle West of the United States*, a work of numbing detail, though possibly of some interest to Mr. Houghton, who always tried to take some profit from the refectory reading. I droned on, no one attending.

"'That was the year in which the International Exposition was held in St. Looee—'"

The pulpit light blinked red, committed. Pause. The sounds of masticating and clashing cutlery slowly ceased. No, he *couldn't*—he *wouldn't*. That wise-ass from New York has been here for over two years. He *knows* it's not St. Looee. The Prefect of Reading is dimly meditating the same thing. It's his move. He's too far in now: the light is lit and I've made no move to correct myself.

"That's St. Louis, of course, Mister." Gambit accepted. I tip my biretta. A fool giggles somewhere. No one else does. There *has* to be more.

"'That was the year in which the International Exposition was held in St. Louis, an event later remembered in the popular song "Meet Me in St. Louis, Louis".'"

Jesuits are cool, very cool. Nobody laughed or even smiled. Some even professed not to notice when the Prefect of Reading was reassigned to the missions in Honduras on the following day.

Jousting. There was a great deal of it in the Jesuit training from the first day of the Novitiate onward. Like Homeric warriors before windy Troy, like the Bedouin on the blasted steppe, we were confined to a social system rigid beyond the dreams of Bushido. We enjoyed the system: it defined the ground of the razzia and dictated the tactics whereby some trifling guerdon might be won. As Jesuits we already *were* the system and so there was little inclination to destroy the very thing that gave us our identity, but as Scholastics, the striving underclass of our society, we all craved a little honor, an elegant move within the system that would provoke an eyebrow arched in admiration at the cleverness of the ploy or the grace of its execution. No harm in scrawling an occasional "Up Ours!" on the invisible walls. Our graffiti were intended to amuse rather than to destroy, or even to undermine, and both the egg thrower and the egg-faced target could afford to smile at the ingenuity of the hit, since it struck the system and not the Life.

In the Novitiate we all thought that the system was

identical with the Life, but as the months and the years turned, the distinction between the two became apparent. The system was no more than a set of traditions, like the siesta and the summer villa, which embalmed, in varying degrees of rigidity, ways of doing things. There were other ways, surely, and as we learned more about the history of the Society of Jesus and came in contact with Jesuits from other places and other lands, we all realized that there was nothing sacred about the prevailing Jesuit mores of here and now. What was sacred was the Rule, which embodied the spirit of the Jesuit life and set forth the general norms of action and attitude that made us all Jesuits.

The Rule dictated silence at most meals, and out of that prescription flowed the customary religious practice of reading at table. But what was read in the refectory and how to assure some degree of literacy in the reader were manifestly grist for the system. So the Prefect of Reading, like the Master of Novices before him and every Father Minister after him, took his chances when he sat down at a baize table with a Scholastic and attempted to deal himself a winning hand out of the system. There were a lot of card sharps out there waiting to trump his ace.

The Provincial visited his subjects in foreign parts every year or so, not to bestow medals for trumped aces but to check on the spiritual and intellectual progress of his charges. His first two visits to St. Louis during my stay there were relatively innocuous, but when he arrived at the beginning of my third year the temperature had changed somewhat. The Affair Buchhasser had taken place and the smoking was weighing heavily upon me. I decided to be direct. "Look, Father, I smoke. I know I'm not supposed to, but I do and I can't stop. I'm wasting time, energy and moral purpose trying to do something I cannot. I am requesting permission to smoke."

This was a little bold, confessing a vice and asking permission to continue it. I reasoned that he would give me and others the permission in a year or so, so why not now? He said he'd think about it.

He did. He gave me the permission—and something more. At the end of their third year of Philosophy the Scholastics normally received Minor Orders, those first, rather remote steps leading to the priesthood. The others did, but I didn't. The reason was never given, but I'm certain the smoking business had something to do with it. The Minor Orders were bestowed on me the following year, so there was no permanent damage. But a message had unmistakably been sent.

My diagnosis was correct. Life was better with the permission. All the nonsense with drafts and locks and typewriter-ribbon cases disappeared. I spent no more time in a semistupor on the roof. I smoked less and had fewer house guests in what had become the New York Hilton. And yet I suspect I had already damaged myself in St. Louis, not in the eyes of the Provincial but in some inner spiritual sense. Despite all the chortling and good-fellow-ship, *Orat pro Soc.* was, after all, a more becoming Jesuit title than *Fumat pro Soc.* Smoking was not prohibited by either natural or divine law. It was merely a disciplinary matter, but its constant, flagrant and willed violations eroded an integral part of the system. It meant that I had consciously given up on something. It was the first time that had happened to me. It was my first conscious surrender, and *that* was important, even though it was apparently cured by a simple permission.

It was close to status time again. The three years of Philosophy were almost over and I would now be assigned to teach in some Jesuit high school. Like all the Philosophers, I possessed a Licentiate in Philosophy, a degree granted us, through a kind of proxy arrangement, by the Pontifical Institute in Rome. When it was conferred there was an interesting and revealing little ceremony in which we took an oath never to teach or publicly embrace any system other than Thomism. But more than the ambivalent and indiscriminate Ph.L., I was the holder of a genuine M.A. in Classics. I had a leg up.

But before I was reassigned, I had to return to my home Province, something I was looking forward to almost as eagerly as I had Vow Day. The appropriate *rites de passage* were performed. Brother Buyer introduced Mr. Wilson, S.J., late of Baltimore, Maryland, and now his designated Imam, to various profitable contacts among the Lay Brothers and the wholesalers of St. Louis. I passed to Jack Flynn a coded copy of Ray Brunschweiger's address. Then Houghton, McGarry and I got back on the Pennsy to rejoin our lost brethren. Brother Buyer, I suspect, *flew* home.

It was a splendid reunion at Woodstock in the Maryland hills. Those who had done Philosophy there had become immensely proficient in golf but were promptly taken to the cleaners at bridge by Brother Buyer. Chuck reappeared from his three-year exile with Matt Leahy in the Chicago Province and broke the Woodstock course record his first time around the links. And he didn't take a shower afterward.

It occurred to me how much I had missed them all, even Chuck. At some hard-to-define point, charity had yielded to genuine comradeship. We all had our friends, but that inner circle was surrounded by ever-widening arcs of men with whom I had shared years of successive and identical experiences. We spoke a very special language shared by no others, and, like veterans of some undeclared war, we greatly rejoiced together in our survival. We discovered in each other qualities unsuspected or unacknowledged in the social furnace of the Novitiate. I glowed to see Matt Leahy and Tom Connolly again. I could look upon Mr. Vogelsinger, S.J., and Mr. Cloney, S.J., and take pleasure in them in a deeper and more heartfelt way than mere charity had ever dictated.

Not all the old faces were present. Inevitably there had been a few more departures in the intervening years. Some I already knew about from the monthly Provincial Newsletter which on occasion carried the terse and inconspicuous notice: "*Litt. dim. acceperunt* . . . The following received their Dismissory Letters . . ." It was a brief and pointed Jesuit epitaph for the living, those who had requested and received formal release from their vows and were already making their uncertain way in the World.

But they were far from my thoughts in that particular June. I and the others sat around and speculated wildly on where we might be sent that exciting summer. This time there would be no requests, and the possibilities were excitingly varied. Regis was my fantasy: to return and dazzle the old alma mater. Even Xavier, the once hateful rival on Sixteenth Street, would be acceptable, if less desirable. Fordham Prep put you on the campus of Fordham University, and that might be interesting. Brooklyn Prep sounded boring, but St. Peter's Prep in Jersey City was developing a kind of underground reputation as an OK place to teach.

The status was posted one morning in June while we were at breakfast. It listed *every* new Jesuit assignment for the following year, but the eagle eye found the appropriate entry soon enough. As I approached the bulletin board, the sea of black robes parted in the awe of the moment. Let him see for himself. There it was, the ultimate, the unspeakable, no, the unthinkable. I was being sent, together with Mr. Charles Gilligan, S.J., to St. Peter Canisius High School in Buffalo, New York— Devil's Island, with a degenerate Vince Lombardi for company.

IX

The Devil's Paradise

When events of great moral import shake the world—the fall of Constantinople to the Turks, the Lisbon earthquake, or a Jesuit's posting in Buffalo—there should be ample time to reflect upon their place in the Divine Plan. My fate was agreeable to most: to the theologians who surmised that by now I must be lying down during meditation to deserve such chastisement; to the pious Buffalonians who were delighted that I should have the chance to get to know better their native city, of which I had so often spoken; to my supposed friends who wallowed in the high, glorious irony of it all; and presumably to my superiors, who did the deed with what one supposes was great, if possibly malicious, intent. It was not agreeable to me, however.

The opportunity for reflection came during villa, celebrated in this summer between Philosophy and Regency on the desolate shores of Lake Champlain. The town, which we never saw, was called Port Kent and it was your perfect Jesuit summer storage, at least until the completion of the ultimate Loyola Villa rumored to be under construction at the headwaters of the Amazon. The new Regents of the New York and Maryland Province were shipped northward by train to join those others who had finished their first or second year of teaching and were even then being dragged, kicking and screaming, to the same piney barren. These latter, you see, had tasted of the World, where softball no longer charmed and long walks pleased not, except they were taken on Manhattan Island between Fifty-seventh and Forty-second on Fifth.

It was at Port Kent that we got the first eyewitness reports on Buffalo, and at first they defied belief: it was going to be all right. That was the word of those already in the embrace of that frigid Erie maiden, and I could see that it did make a certain crude sense. For years Buffalo had been used precisely as a kind of Devil's Island, a penal colony for the fractious, the far out and the farfetched among the Scholastic population. But in so skewing its demography, the Provincial had unwittingly succeeded in converting a prison into a wildlife sanctuary. Buffalo was filled with all my old friends.

That was cheering news; how true it was remained to be seen. For two weeks meanwhile we renewed old ties, an agreeable pastime, and then made our annual retreat. Lately the Spiritual Exercises were being given to us by elderly Spiritual Fathers or, worse, by ancient warhorses from one or other of the Jesuit houses where retreats were laid like healing balm upon the souls of innocent laymen. The clarion call to repentance and self-reformation, which might have worked wonders upon the consciences of impressionable Externs, got only a sluggish reaction from Scholastics, who by then had dutifully responded to every spiritual alarum sounded since the days of Saint Paul. We attended good-naturedly nonetheless, almost as if we feared that our inattention might cause those antique Savonarolas to lose their jobs.

Then fell the terrible blow. Immediately after the retreat, all those prudent or devious enough to have argued that summer school at Fordham was an absolute necessity to their intellectual development were loaded like suddenly released prisoners of war onto the New York Central and went cheering off to New York City. As the train's echoes died away, the loungers around Port Kent Station could now hear quite plainly another sound. "Why, those nice boys from Loyola Villa are shouting filthy things at those other nice boys who just left on the New York train!" In the best tradition of civilized society, the women and children, the wounded, maimed and halt, Brother Buyer well forward in their number, had all been evacuated; the rest of us turned in our Bataan death trap to face the foe.

The foe was six more weeks of listless and empty boredom in that wretched place. We sat on rustic furniture on the crumbling porches of one more set of frame bungalows and dully contemplated Lake Champlain and the possibility of a quick death beneath its frigid black waves. The softball field resembled an overgrown grave-yard, and not even Chuck's prodigious recruiting got an appropriate number of bodies onto its lumpy surface. There were morose games of Ping-Pong, dull detective stories, a radio and an occasional bland movie to amuse us and some classes to instruct us. The mood was murderously sullen, rebellious, and even then I guessed that at least one part of the Jesuit system was rapidly outliving its usefulness.

By then we all knew what we would be teaching in the following fall and were accordingly assigned to some harmless pedagogical exercises in the hope that we might do a creditable job. I was supposed to teach Latin, French and English to the seniors at Canisius High School, and so I was handed over to the ministrations of the Reverend Raphael Mere, S.J., who was to make a Latin IV teacher of me, J. Ashton Donleavy and Emile LaPlante. It was another marvelous Jesuit melange, and its comic unlikeliness probably carried me through that deadly siege of Port Kent.

We three fellow Regents had never seen one another before. Jim Donleavy was from Baltimore, a quiet, pale-eyed young man with no shoulders and no chin but a deliciously wicked sense of humor. Mealy LaPlante, my first encounter with anyone from the New Orleans Province, was a darkly effete Southern hysteric in the grand tradition who, if he had not been a Jesuit, would doubtless have been running an elegant bordello or slowly dying of a venereal disease in a mossy bayou. We all learned to say "sheet" at Mealy's unathletic knee and marveled at the unfailing aptness of his use of "sheet-haid," his favorite and almost exclusive epithet for man and mammal.

It was Mealy who came up with "Père Mère," and we used no other name for our mentor. Père Mère was a kind of courtly cipher who managed to stretch good manners into a perfectly acceptable substitute for intelligence, understanding, wisdom or wit. He was a harmless, perhaps even a good man who had sunk to his appropriate Jesuit niche at something called the Loyola School, a kind of genteel high school that Ours ran on Park Avenue for the sole benefit, it seemed, of wealthy South Americans, and very few of them at that. So Père Mère earned his winter keep by teaching Latin IV to the sons of an Argentine diplomat and a Nicaraguan embezzler, and summers journeyed north, far out of harm's way, to pass on his expertise to new Regents. His mere voluntary presence at the despicable Port Kent said everything that needed saying about him.

Père Mère regaled us daily with stories about the extraordinary difficulties that he faced in teaching two rich South American adolescents, and how he had risen to new pedagogical heights in forming them into classical scholars. Unfortunately for Père Mère, we had all been to high school, and so we listened with amazement and disbelief, turned away from open derision only by his mild manner and unassuming tone. None of us had ever stood before a class, and yet we knew that wherever we were and whatever we did, we would never share the placid and undisturbed life of Père Mère. But to fill the time and explore the possibility of tipping him into at least a mild fret, we invented out of our own rapidly crumbling imaginations every conceivable classroom emergency from aphasia and epileptic attack to the total collapse of Western civilization. He smiled his mild smile and counseled that patience and good manners might solve any ill.

Jim Donleavy sat quietly and observed this extraordinary performance through those wondering pale eyes; we would find out later what he was thinking. Mealy knew no such moderation. He sat and twisted and muttered "Sheethaid" with metronomic regularity for two hours, whether at me for his own amusement or at Père Mère by way of comment, I could not tell. Possibly both. Between epithets Mealy would raise his voice a little and in his creamiest Southern style pose *le bon* Père Mère yet another academic, legal, moral and metaphysical conundrum of such great complexity and so little likelihood that I began to suspect that the syphilis had in fact reached his brain. Père Mère could not be drawn from out of his own dim perspectives, and Mealy marched his two companions up and down the pebbly beach for hours afterward discoursing in his foul but charming way on the possibility of a joint—but anonymous—letter to the Father General manifesting Père Mère for sodomizing a sheep without permission and recreating out of the assigned times.

My new principal, Father Donald Kurtz, arrived at Port Kent to check out his new acquisitions and count his old ones. He told me to pay close attention to Père Mère, and I swore I was (I could hear the hiss of "Sheethaid" from behind a newspaper nearby). I resisted the temptation to tell *him* to pay close attention to Mr. Gilligan, since that was likely to be even more rewarding. But I did conceive a rather daring plan. I begged Father Kurtz that I might be permitted to leave Port Kent early and spend a few days in Quebec to improve my French accent. The proposition was ludicrous—nothing short of a pharyngotomy would have improved my French accent—but I was resolved to get out of there and so why not? "Sheet," commented

Mealy, who was even then thinking of writing to his Provincial for a few days at Tulane to improve his football coaching.

Whatever its consistency, it worked. We had an extravagant private party to celebrate my *coup de langue,* and the revelry and beer drinking ran far into the night, so far, in fact, that I slept through my alarm the next morning. The train to Montreal was due at eight, and Mealy found me still sleeping at seven-thirty. "Sheethaid," he screamed, "yo gonna blow it." Not on your life. Half dressed, half shaved and only half awake, I was shoved into a jeep, carried to the station and hoisted onto the slowly departing train. I didn't quite catch Mealy's last word, but I did get off the train at Rouse's Point and send him his very first collect telegram: "Pay attention to Père Mère and don't forget to use your salve."

Based on the single, though illuminating, St. Louis experience, I had conceived a deep suspicion of anyplace that called itself the Queen City of anything. Now at last we were all assembled in the Queen City of the Lakes, a dubious title that Buffalo shared, without acrimony, with Cleveland. "At least you weren't sent to Cleveland," I had been told at Port Kent by someone who knew full well that the only reason I wasn't was because Cleveland wasn't in the New York Province. No, I wasn't sent to Cleveland, but I had gotten the next worst thing.

Or so I was convinced. But as I regarded our number I conceded I could be wrong. Chuck, I discovered, no longer bothered me, and his claim to have graded three hundred exams in fifteen minutes was now merely zany.

And he could now work off his physical energies with teenage jocks, who thought he was neat, if a little filthy. Singlefinger was there, too, but after all he was now, by common consent, one hundred and fifty-seven years old, and the Provincial probably wanted him to die—or disintegrate—on his native tundra.

The rest were all old friends: Jack Scally, my constant consolation from St. Louis and beyond (Jack Flynn would follow next year); Joe Murphy, who had already nicely calculated the dimensions of this thing called the Jesuit life and was on top of it, and who would quite predictably move, if not to its very summit, then smoothly and gracefully along its high roads; Jim Haggerty, the grand archivist of Province gossip and lore who was already so dedicated to his special calling that he would spend hours propping up the centennial Father Archer (only Haggerty knew that he used to be called Bogenschütz) in a corner and extracting from him the least detail of the Great War of the German-Speaking and English-Speaking Fathers on the Buffalo Mission; Dan Meeker, whose path through our midst was so purposefully rapid and yet enigmatic that no one knew whither he was hurrying or why.

Canisius High School was located on pleasant, tree-lined Delaware Avenue, and it has the distinction of being the only *new* Jesuit house I have ever entered. The classroom building, at least. This was flanked on one side by a former Masonic auditorium and mansion, now under devious Jesuit control, and on the other by an old house where President McKinley had died in 1901 at an assassin's hand. All were now part of the Jesuit high school: the Fathers laid the ghost of the Masons in the mansion, where the chapel and the recreation rooms were also located, while the Scholastics grappled with the spirit of McKinley on the other side of the lawn.

Walking back into a Jesuit high-school classroom after seven years elicited an immediate and powerful sense of déjà vu. There was a young ice skater who showed up at Canisius every winter for a couple of weeks. He was in the national company of Ice Capades and was finishing his education by popping in and out of Jesuit high schools from California to New York, and with little or no interruption of either matter or style. And no wonder. The tradition carried all of us along in its grip, one generation educating the next. I learned the style from my teachers at Regis, and now I was about to impart it to an entire new generation of students at Canisius, some of whom would doubtless become Jesuits, *in saecula saeculorum.*

I stood there in my black robe of authority with twenty-five years of life and four hundred years of tradition behind me and silently surveyed my charges. I had at hand a number of opening-day ploys inherited from four years of opening-day theatrics at Regis. I sat down and stared at the thirty-five seniors before me. They too had been through this before and awaited my opening move. I was strongly tempted to say, "Boys, if there are any problems about taking a bath, see me in private." No, save that for a more desperate moment. I looked down at the role book. Aguilar? Where did he come from? Brice, Brzoska, Czeislar, Czerewski, Dlugas, Dumbrowski, Gaglione—on and on they went, names without vowels with a sprinkling of more familiar Italian and Irish ethnics. The Italians were football players; the Irish, basketballers. The vowelless wonders were Poles, who played no sports but rested tranquil in the knowledge that tney were in the overwhelming majority. I decided not to call the roll.

I spied my first target. An ageless Jesuit tradition was the beadle, an appointed student functionary in each class who sat next to the door, took care of the general housekeeping, informed on or petitioned for the other students as required, and served as either court jester or moral exemplar, bright or vile.

"What's your name?"

"Juliano, Mister."

"And what's your last name?"

"Juliano, Mister." Service returned, feebly, but returned.

"Ah, well, then, Mr. Juliano, what's your idea of the duties of a beadle?"

"To serve and be amusing, Mister." This kid *wanted* the job.

"Be amusing, Juliano."

"We were all due at assembly ten minutes ago, Mister." He was hired. And he served in his amusing way for an entire year despite daily threats of dismissal from his sinecure for his frequent offenses of *lèse majesté*.

Juliano proved his worth very quickly. Each classroom was connected to the principal's office by a two-way intercom system, and it was the custom of the good Father Kurtz to abuse the system on occasion by listening in on classes unannounced. But Juliano was too fast for him. His ears were perfectly attuned to the slight telltale click from the box on the wall. His accusing hand shot immediately toward the intercom, and his lips silently formed the words "The Box. The Box." I immediately interrupted my story of what it was like when *I* played football and we fell to parsing like grammarians possessed until Juliano signaled the sign-off click. Father Kurtz was not a big fan of parsing.

Teaching high school was extremely hard work, I discovered. I was responsible for both the learning and the good order of my students; in the Jesuit system the two were closely intertwined. So I drilled in Vergil, tried to keep the aisles straight and mayhem at bay and both them and me amused in a single, simultaneous and unlikely triple play. I spent entire weekends reading their English compositions and every night correcting their French half-sheets. They and I met once every day, sometimes twice a day, from September to June, a long cohabitation. By March tempers and good humor were frayed on both sides.

But it was rewarding. The educational changes rung on a high-school student are visible and therefore gratifying. Some of them blossomed before my eyes: Aguilar was writing poetry before February, and Podlecki soon mastered every nuance of the Greek genitive, subjective and objective, of separation, of description, of alleged parentage, of surreptitious departure, of libelous imputation and all the other species I had coolly invented for his edification. Even an occasional football player was heard to grunt something about college in terms other than athletic scholarships.

Regis was not a red-hot sports school; its forte was its

dramatic and debating societies. Canisius, on the other hand, was perennial city champion in football and basket-ball, and so its halls were filled with the unaccustomed forms of swaggering hulks, some very wide and some exceedingly tall. The athletes were not very bright as a group, but they held their own in class, even in the face of endless practice sessions.

That fall I went to my first high-school pep rally and football game, when the Canisius Crusaders took on the cretinous warriors fielded by the Franciscans. "And Grey Franciscans, at that," Haggerty muttered derisively, with a perfect mastery, if not of football, then of the innumera-ble, subtle and quite meaningless distinctions among Franciscans. *Non patitur distinctionem bestialitas,* as Thomas was wont to say of other matters. It was fiercely exciting, and the pleasure of watching my children grind those mindless Franciscan helots into the frozen turf uncovered a new and unsuspected vein of sadism in my Jesuit soul. I could not even survive the basketball season. At one close game I found myself suspended somewhere between an anxiety attack and cardiac arrest, and I vowed then and there that the boys would have to finish the season without my encouraging presence.

The Scholastics lived a busy but pleasant life. After a day in the classroom we dined in the elegant refectory, where all meals were served by what was reputed to be a former Hungarian count, complete with dueling scar, whose aspect was so terrifying that he had cowed tiny and nervous Father Fusarillo into ordering the same unap-petizing breakfast every day for six years. After dinner the Fathers went to their recreation room to watch television and we to ours to correct papers and listen to Chuck and/ or the largest collection of Joni James records on the Western Tier. We could, if we wished, join the Fathers at their TV—they apparently never graded papers, though they taught the same subjects as we—but frequently the conversation was more pleasant in our own quarters. We discussed nothing but the students.

Later in the evening, when the Count had safely departed, we could go down to the kitchen and have a beer if we wished. The kitchen and the beer were presided over, night after night, by the good Father known to us as Dollar Bill—so called from his custom of marking his place in his breviary with a crisp bill—who was, quite incredibly, the Spiritual Father of the students and the chief fund-raiser of the community. It was on one of those evenings that I was truly scandalized for the first and only time in my life: Dollar Bill, deep in his cups, regaled us with the rather innocent sex habits of one of the students, and by name, a piece of information he almost certainly had to have heard in confession. And if there was anything sacred in the Catholic Church, it was the Seal of Confession.

Dollar Bill was a vicious and abominable man, one of the very few I ever met in the Society, and the Scholastics instinctively gave him a wide berth, all save Chuck, who would talk to anyone who stood in place for longer than thirty seconds. But I inadvertently stumbled over him on one occasion. The Fathers had what were known as "caves," the homes of friendly Externs whom they cultivated, where they were often invited for dinner and other entertainments. Scholastics were not supposed to have "caves," though it was suspected that Joe Murphy was hollowing out what was still only a small hole somewhere in East Aurora, and so it was only we, the Rector, who had professional obligation to set a good example, and Father Fusarillo who was afraid the Count would note his absence, who sat down to community dinner in the refectory on Thanksgiving, Christmas and a great many Sundays during the year.

Perhaps it was just as well that we did not go into company very often. On one occasion a number of the Scholastics were invited to a butlered dinner by a well-settled lady of some seventy-odd summers who either felt sorry for us or else confused us with Fathers. Chuck was sitting, or had seated himself, at our hostess' right hand. I listened with disbelief from the other end of the table as Chuck harangued that gentle dame with the virtues of a wishbone versus a flanker back offense, generously glossed from the recent history of the Buffalo Bills, who she doubtless thought were some kind of game birds. Now in full flight, Chuck reverted to an old Novitiate habit. Without breaking his verbal stride or losing the thread of his devastating argument, he took up his napkin and began robustly to polish his still-unused silverware. The lady was also a pro. Without uttering a word or even removing her fixed gaze from Chuck's hoarsely blithering mouth, she contrived to signal her butler, who silently but disapprovingly changed *all* the silver on the table. The despised Kempis had said it well: "I would that many a time I had not been in company." Chuck's.

Each Father's "cave" was, of course, off limits to everyone else and *a fortiori* to Scholastics, who were supposed to be home in bed in any event. After a football game one of my students asked if he might drive me home, and on the way we stopped off at his house to say hello to his parents. His parents were otherwise engaged, with Dollar Bill, as it turned out, who was ensconced there in his "cave" with his suit jacket and clerical collar off and with an extremely large scotch and water in his uncertain hand. It was the shortest greeting on record, more like a "he—" than a "hello," as I backed out the door. I could only hope that he was too drunk to notice or remember.

Dollar Bill was an exception. In that small community the gap between Fathers and Scholastics had noticeably lessened, particularly since the age difference was narrowing down to less than ten years in some instances. The Rector was still the Rector, but even he could be addressed, only by an urgent insistence on his part, on a first-name basis. Otherwise, the relationships were easy and familiar. The younger Fathers and the Scholastics drank together and sometimes went out together, and we shared the students at the center of our interests. Socially, at least, the priesthood no longer seemed so remote. I could almost imagine being one of them.

In Buffalo the Scholastics lived on a rather long leash. Unlike our peers in New York City, who always wore clerical garb, we could go out into the city in mufti, or, rather, quasi-mufti since we had sports shirts and wind-breakers but no slacks, and the black trousers and shoes must have proclaimed what we were more obviously than if we had been wearing phylacteries bound around our brows. As a group we had access to one of the community cars, and early on we made the obligatory pilgrimage to Niagara Falls, where Finglefanger, now entirely unprotected by Sacred Silence, discoursed at length on kilowatts and cubic tons of water to his usual unappreciative audience. We could even take the car at night to drive-ins, where we amazedly watched everything from *Beach Blanket Bingo* to the dubious historical lessons of *O.K., Nero,* a piece of Italian claptrap unredeemed by anything save the luridly massive breasts of Silvana Pampanini.

Buffalo was my first real taste of the World after seven years of relatively severe seclusion. After a few cautious bites, I concluded that I liked it, even in its diminished Buffalo version. The World did not impress me as either dangerous or immoral; indeed, it appeared, from my admittedly peculiar perspective, a very Catholic place. I came to know Externs, most of whom were kind and decent people who had, moreover, a quite staggering respect for the clerical estate. They didn't even seem to care that we were only Scholastics; our clothes and position proclaimed that we were God's men, and that was enough. We were also the teachers of their children in many instances, and through their eyes I began to form my first dim and exceedingly remote vision of what it must be like to be a parent. And many of them appeared to be of the opposite sex.

It was only later that I noticed that we were never exposed to a large and interesting segment of the female population, to wit, unmarried women between eighteen and forty. I met only the girl friends and mothers of my students, and those only in the most public of circumstances. Their mothers, I noted with some interest, were no longer quite old enough to be *my* mother. I looked and they looked, and though Joe Murphy maliciously claimed that I had reinvented the bell curve by grading the students according to the cup size of their mothers' bras, those good ladies kept themselves a healthy if not an awesome distance from the Jesuit Mister from New York. And they kindled no notable erotic fires in the same Mister's fertile imagination. Nobody's clothes got torn off, either at Parents' Night or when I was alone in my own room.

Our quarters were typical Jesuit rooms of the Scholastic variety: bed, desk, armoire (had Saint Ignatius been early frightened in a closet?), bookcase and prie-dieu. But now there were differences. I now had a radio and we no longer cleaned our own rooms or made our own beds. These tasks were performed by Ralph and Roy, two middle-aged Extern gentlemen of a very different sexual preference who obviously enjoyed chattering side by side through the Sheraton-McKinley making beds and dusting prie-dieus. We joked about them in a kind of affectionate way. They professed to notice us not at all.

It was at Buffalo I discovered I was a night person, and somewhat more besides. It is a harmless thing, being a night person, whether by metabolism or by choice. But whoever is a night person is necessarily not a morning person. We were still supposed to rise at 5:30 A.M. and meditate between 6 and 7 before Mass and breakfast. But if I stayed up until 1 or 2 A.M. talking or listening to the radio, there was no likely way I was going to get up at 5:30 and begin meditating at 6. I began sleeping into meditation, and then finally *through* meditation, and rising with only the greatest difficulty, and then not always, for Mass at 7 A.M. Like smoking, this was another surrender. But the first was only a matter of discipline; meditation was the chief spiritual exercise of the day, and to surrender on that front was to cut something out of the core of being a Jesuit. And this time no one could or would give me permission.

This was probably the end of me as a Jesuit, though I did not think of it as such at that time. I still lived the life of the vows, but all the spiritual underpinning had been stripped away. I was by then a "natural" Jesuit; I unreflectively took what I liked about the life: the teaching, the study, the comradeship, the lack of material concerns. The "spiritual" Jesuit had almost vanished, his entrails all but rotted away.

Unexpectedly, I enjoyed my two years at Buffalo, chiefly because I loved the classroom. And I was a first-rate teacher: I cared for the students and the subjects. The community at Canisius was friendly and relaxed—no wonder, we lived quite a comfortable life—and the students were outgoing, enthusiastic and admiring. And the future was equally bright. By now there was no doubt in my mind that I could have my choice of career in that least Society, likely as a university professor, in history perhaps, or patristics or Scripture. Rome beckoned, unmistakably. There was nothing that stood between me and whatever Ultimate Laurels the Society of Jesus might choose to bestow, none save the fact that I no longer had a vocation.

I had had a vocation, not to the priesthood certainly,

not to the spiritual life, not even to the religious life perhaps, but to the Jesuits. I had become a Jesuit and discovered over many years that that calling was more complex than I was and made more demands than I could possibly fulfill. I would have made a good soldier or a good professor, but never a proper Jesuit. Half-man and half-angel was not my métier. So long as the angelic side was translated into mere observance, as it was in the Novitiate, I could soar a little on my ersatz wings. But once those concrete pylons, which had once seemed so painful, were removed from under and around me, I began my slow glide to earth, a splendid black eagle that could not, alas, fly.

I did not discover that sad fact at Buffalo, though it was doubtless true even then. At the end of my second year of teaching, the Provincial decided that I was to be given a whole bushel of plums. My teaching was cut short and I was sent to the University of Louvain to get my Ph.D. and then stay on and do Theology somewhere else in Europe, at Paris, perhaps, or Rome. I was fully ambitious enough to know what that meant. I packed and sailed to Europe, just like that, for how long I had no idea nor any care. But the effect was quite different from what I expected. I was now alone, remote from all the friends and familiar surroundings that had cushioned me from thought and reflection. At last I came face to face with myself.

It is not easy to sort it out now, how such an immense decision was taken so quickly and with so little apparent effort. Perhaps I had never given myself and so there was no pain in taking myself back. There was no soul-searching, no torment or even ambivalence. Two weeks after arriving at the Jesuit house on Minderbroedersstraat in Louvain, I awoke one morning with the absolute conviction that this was not for me, nor I for it.

The recommended Jesuit posture for contemplating such decisions was to place oneself on one's deathbed. Only thus, counseled Saint Ignatius, would one more likely choose the greater good. I did not lie down. Instead, I went directly to the room of one of the American Fathers doing his doctoral studies in that same house. Nothing in his Jesuit training had prepared Robert Dolan for this particular task, for directing the conscience of someone down the hall who was preparing to change his life in a way neither of them fully understood. Nor was I sure what, if anything, I was asking him. I had decided to leave and I had to tell someone. By sheerest chance, Robert Dolan, S.J., was it.

He listened in silence, a small smile upon his lips, while little fear lines spread in networks around the corners of his eyes. Outside, it was raining on Minderbroedersstraat, as it did almost every day. I could not stand the pain in Dolan's face one moment longer, the pain I was causing him by this unexpected and undeserved revelation from a stranger. I turned and stared out at the wet cobblestones. My own anxiety was rising. I had heard myself saying in a quite matter-of-fact manner things I had not dared utter even to myself for nine years. We sat awkwardly for a minute.

"You know," he said, "my brother runs a shipping company in New York. Maybe he can help you with a job afterward." A what?

Whatever was going to happen to me was not going to happen to me there in Provincia Belgica Septentrionalis. I explained my intentions to the Rector of the house. He was not very disturbed, nor should he have been. I belonged to someone else, the New York Province, and so obviously I should return there. Tickets were provided on what seemed like the very next flight from Brussels to New York, and I was instructed by cable to report to the "College of St. Ignatius" in Manhasset, the infamous Inisfada.

I spent three weeks in that most peculiar of Jesuit houses. How many of us there were I cannot tell, twelve, fifteen, twenty perhaps, since attendance at anything that might be called "common exercises" was erratic, to say the least. I got out of the house as often as I could, on sad journeys to the Bronx to mend only half-concealed broken hearts. But I lived, nonetheless, there at Inisfada amidst depressing human ruins.

Elderly Jesuits were not sent to Inisfada to die; they went to their end more graciously, surrounded by the newest and youngest recruits of the Society at St. Andrew on Hudson, and were buried in the quiet and impressive cemetery there. Inisfada was only for dead aspirations and hopes, dreams that had expired in a haze of alcohol, ideals crushed by an intolerable burden of weariness or despair. The fortunate in that unfortunate company were those of us who were simply waiting for a piece of paper from Rome that would signal release and perhaps new hopes and new aspirations.

Inisfada was like a second Long Retreat, a swift and painful regression along that same Jesuit path I had come.

It was a surreal rite of passage, not into the World but out of the past. Parting from friends would have been unbearable, but I had nothing in common with these cruel parodies of Jesuits. I did not depart in tears; I fled in terror.

When I reflect upon my decision, it seems like a gift, a sudden and undeserved *coup de grace* which restored me to myself and allowed me to escape early from the unreflective hypocrisy into which I had slipped and which would almost certainly have had sad and terrible personal consequences in the following Jesuit years.

If it was a gift, I am grateful. I am grateful, too, that it came when it did. I had been permitted to enjoy the best moments of being a Jesuit, of tasting something quite remarkable and of walking away with the savor still sweet in my mouth. More, I still think Jesuit thoughts and urge attractive and quite specious Jesuit arguments on all who will attend. I view life through Jesuit eyes and greet it with Jesuit laughter. Sans vows. Sans prayer. Sans faith. Sans everything except gratitude.

Gratias

About the Author

F. E. Peters:

Dir.stud.Prox.Orient.in univ.N.Y.U.,
doc.hist.,rel.isl.,phil.in schol.
grad.et coll.an.19 mag., litt.dim.acc.,
nupt.et pater an.22, exspect.destin
et orat pro Soc.